How To Talk To Anyone

From Small Talk to Big Impact

Communicate with confidence,
create instant connection and master
every social & professional conversation
even if you're an introvert!

Anne McKeown

©Copyright Anne McKeown 2025 - All rights reserved.

The content within this book may not be reproduced, duplicated or transmitted without direct written permission from the author or the publisher.

Under no circumstances will any blame or legal responsibility be held against the publisher or author for any damages, reparation, or monetary loss due to the information contained within this book. Either directly or indirectly. You are responsible for your own choices, actions, and results.

Legal Notice:

This book is copyright-protected. This book is only for personal use. You cannot amend, distribute, sell, use, quote or paraphrase any part of the content within this book without the consent of the author or publisher.

Disclaimer Notice:

Please note the information contained within this document is for educational and entertainment purposes only. We have made every effort to present accurate, up-to-date, and reliable information. No warranties of any kind are declared or implied. Readers acknowledge that the author is not engaging in the rendering of legal, financial, medical or professional advice. The content within this book has been derived from various sources. Please consult a licensed professional before attempting any techniques outlined in this book.

By reading this document, the reader agrees that under no circumstances is the author responsible for any losses, direct or indirect, which are incurred as a result of the use of the information contained within this document, including, but not limited to, — errors, omissions, or inaccuracies.

Contents

1. Introduction to Powerful Interactions — 1
2. Managing Social Anxiety — 5
3. Building a Foundation of Confidence — 14
4. Mastering Small Talk — 28
5. De-coding Non-Verbal Communication — 38
6. Empathy and Active Listening — 49
7. Balancing Speaking and Listening — 59
8. Networking and Career Advancement — 70
9. Enhancing Memory and Recall — 79
10. Cultural Sensitivity in Communication — 88
11. Special Considerations for Introverts — 99
12. Advanced Psychological Insights — 109
13. Sustaining Long-Term Growth and Connection — 118
14. Final Word — 129
15. Make a Difference with Your Review and Unlock the Power of Connection — 131
16. References — 134

1

INTRODUCTION TO POWERFUL INTERACTIONS

"Be who you are and speak from your guts and heart. It's all one has."
Hubert Humphrey

Communication is at the heart of human interaction, yet it remains an area where many of us stumble. Whether at work or in social settings, we can often find ourselves on the outside looking in, unsure of how to connect.

Many years ago, not long after starting a new job, I was invited to a drinks evening with colleagues who had worked together for many years. I remember entering the room and feeling hesitant. I hovered at the edge of the conversation, wrestling with the dilemma: how do I break into this circle? This simple yet profound moment sent me down the path of learning everything I could about communication and social skills.

This book is about those moments. It's about the fear of rejection that keeps us silent, the awkwardness of small talk that makes us stumble, and the misreading of social cues that can lead to misunderstandings. I've repeatedly seen people struggle with these challenges in my many years as a communications coach. Anxiety does not discriminate; it affects corporate leaders, small business owners, and individuals from all walks of life. I know because I've coached them!

My goal with this book is clear: to equip you with practical tools and techniques to communicate with confidence. I want you to create connections that feel genuine and for you to enjoy every interaction, whether it's a casual chat or a critical business meeting. This is not just about talking to anyone; it's about feeling good while doing it.

Let me introduce myself. I'm Anne McKeown, and I've dedicated my career to helping people like you step up, speak up, and show up with confidence. Communication is not a one-size-fits-all skill. It requires understanding your strengths, your fears and your unique voice.

Here are some questions clients have asked me and I've answered throughout this book:

- What techniques can help me manage anxiety during important social interactions?

- How do I make a memorable impression when meeting someone new?

- What are some effective conversation starters for networking events?

- How can I keep a conversation flowing naturally without awkward pauses?

- What strategies can I use to overcome my fear of speaking up in meetings?

- How do I read body language to understand what someone is really thinking?

- What are practical ways to boost my self-confidence in social settings?

- How do I connect on a deeper level with acquaintances and build lasting relationships?

- How can I handle miscommunications or misunderstandings?

- What tips can help me remember names and details about people I meet?

- How do I engage introverted individuals in conversation without overwhelming them?

- What are the best ways to express disagreement without causing conflict?

- How can I tailor my communication style to suit different cultural contexts?

- What should I do if I feel ignored or unheard in a group discussion?

- How do I politely exit a conversation that isn't going well?

If you aspire to connect more deeply with others, to be heard and understood, discover your unique communication style, build your inner confidence and manage social anxiety then this book is for you.

If you are looking to grow personally and professionally, want to master small talk, understand body language, emotional intelligence, attentive listening and networking with ease, look no further.

Each chapter builds on the next and provides insights and strategies tailored to your needs. Whether you're an introvert seeking to navigate extroverted spaces or someone looking to refine your communication skills, there's something here for you.

What sets this book apart is its focus on authenticity. We won't just skim the surface; we'll dive deep into what makes communication meaningful. We'll explore strategies that honor who you are, especially if you're more reserved. You'll learn to communicate in a way that feels true to you.

ANNE MCKEOWN

As we begin, I invite you to see this as more than a book. It's a step-by-step guide, a companion and a source of encouragement.

Let's start this journey together.

2

MANAGING SOCIAL ANXIETY

"Communication is a dance between risk and reward." Anne McKeown

This chapter delves into the multifaceted topic of social anxiety, exploring its origins and manifestations. We look at the genetic and experiential factors that shape it, recognize the societal pressures that amplify it, and introduce the self-awareness needed to navigate it. This journey of understanding lays the foundation for a deeper exploration of techniques and strategies designed to manage and alleviate the impact of social anxiety.

For many, the anticipation of social interactions triggers a flow of physiological reactions that can feel overwhelming. Sweaty palms, a racing heart, and an inexplicable urge to flee are common indications of this invisible burden. Though often unseen by others, these symptoms can significantly influence your life. They can lead to avoidance behaviors, where the desire to escape discomfort overrides the opportunity to connect.

Understanding the roots of social anxiety requires looking at both genetic and environmental factors. Research, including a significant genome-wide association study[1] highlights that social anxiety is often inherited and linked to neurobehavioral traits. Some individuals are naturally more sensitive or introverted, making them more susceptible to anxiety in social settings. Yet, genetics is only a part of the puzzle. Past social experiences also play a crucial role. Negative encounters, such as bullying or rejection, can imprint lasting scars, reinforcing the fear of future interactions. These experiences shape our social blueprint, dictating how we perceive and respond to the world around us.

Societal and cultural influences can further compound these challenges. We live in an era where social media dictates norms and shapes self-perception[2]. Many social media platforms offer curated glimpses of idealized lives, amplifying the pressure to conform. This digital arena blurs the line between genuine connection and superficial interaction. For those with social anxiety, the constant comparison to seemingly perfect lives can exacerbate feelings of inadequacy and fear. The need to project a polished image online often leads to a disconnect between one's true self and the persona they present, further fuelling anxiety. Additionally, cultural expectations often demand adherence to specific behaviors, pressuring individuals to navigate social norms that may not align with their natural personality.

Self-awareness becomes a vital tool in managing these complex layers of social anxiety. It begins with recognizing your patterns and triggers. Are there specific situations that heighten your anxiety? Do certain people or environments make you feel more vulnerable? I recommend documenting your experiences to track these triggers and creating a record to help you identify patterns and recurring themes. Set aside dedicated time each day to journal about your social interactions. Focus on moments that felt particularly challenging. What were the circumstances? Who was involved? How did your body react? Over time, this practice will reveal underlying patterns, offering a roadmap to better understand and manage your anxiety. Reflective practices, such as meditation or quiet contemplation, also offer a space to explore these insights further. They encourage a deeper understanding of your responses and help foster a mindset of acceptance and growth. Mindfulness can also be a powerful ally against anxiety, providing a buffer against the stresses that accompany social interactions.

Mindfulness Techniques for Anxiety Reduction

Imagine you are in a busy room with conversations swirling around you. Your thoughts race, and your breathing quickens, but amid this chaos, there's a tool that can help stabalize you: mindfulness.

At its core, mindfulness is about being present, truly present, in the moment. It involves paying attention to your thoughts and feelings without judgment, allowing you to experience them without being overwhelmed. It encourages a state of calm and clarity, enabling you to navigate social engagements with greater ease. The principles of mindfulness focus on grounding yourself in the present moment, which can significantly reduce anxiety. By centering your attention on the here and now, mindfulness helps break the cycle of relentless worry about what might happen or what others might think.

Deep Breathing

It's easy to integrate simple mindfulness exercises into your daily life. One such exercise is deep breathing. When anxiety strikes, your breath often becomes shallow and rapid, exacerbating feelings of panic. By consciously slowing and deepening your breath, you signal your body to relax, reducing physical symptoms of anxiety. Try inhaling deeply through your nose, holding your breath for a count of four, and exhaling slowly through your mouth. Talk to yourself when doing this, say "I am breathing in calm." Then, "I am breathing out peace." This simple practice can help calm your nerves, allowing you to regain control.

Grounding Techniques

Grounding techniques play a crucial role in anchoring your attention. When you feel overwhelmed, focus on your surroundings. Notice the texture of the chair you're sitting in, the sensation of your feet on the ground, or the sounds around you. These techniques divert your mind from anxious thoughts, helping you remain in the present moment.

Self-Compassion

Mindfulness isn't just about reducing anxiety; it also fosters self-compassion. As you practice mindfulness, you learn to view your thoughts and feelings with a non-judgmental mindset. This shift in perspective encourages a kinder relationship with yourself. Instead of berating yourself for having anxious thoughts, you begin to accept them as part of your experience without letting them define you. Developing self-compassion involves exercises that promote self-acceptance and understanding. One approach is to practice self-kindness. When you notice a critical thought, pause and consider how you would respond to a friend in the same situation. Offer yourself the same empathy and support you'd extend to others. Over time, this practice builds a reservoir of self-compassion, reducing the impact of anxiety on your self-esteem.

Incorporating mindfulness into your daily routine can transform how you experience social interactions. Consider setting aside time each day for meditation or reflection. This practice doesn't have to be lengthy; even five minutes of focused breathing or mindful observation can set a positive tone for your day. As you do your daily tasks, look for opportunities to infuse mindfulness into routine activities. Whether it's savoring the taste of your morning coffee, feeling the water on your skin in the shower, or listening to a loved one, these mindful moments can create pockets of calm throughout your day. By making mindfulness a regular part of your life, you cultivate a sense of peace and presence that extends beyond individual exercises, ultimately enhancing your ability to manage anxiety in all areas of your life.

Strategies for Building Social Confidence

Imagine for a moment your thoughts are the scriptwriters of your life. They craft narratives about your interactions, shaping how you feel and act. As a coach, I help people manage their anxiety by teaching various techniques; one such method is altering these scripts. I examine the intricate relationship between your thoughts, feelings, and behaviors. For instance, consider how a thought like, "I'm going to embarrass myself," can spiral into feelings of panic, leading you to avoid speaking up. We can work together to identify these negative thought patterns, challenging their accuracy and reframing them into supportive, realistic appraisals.

Thought Stopping

Another simple technique is referred to as thought-stopping. This involves mentally halting negative thoughts as they arise. Picture yourself watching a movie on TV where the story is becoming dark and negative. It makes you feel anxious; you don't want to see the ending. All you have to do is take the remote control and press the pause button. By recognizing these thoughts early, you can disrupt the cycle of negativity before it escalates.

Exposure Therapy

A technique, known as exposure therapy, is a method that involves gradually facing anxiety-inducing situations to build confidence. Imagine creating a ladder of social challenges, each rung representing a different level of anxiety. Start by listing situations that trigger your anxiety, ranking them from least to most intimidating. For instance, if public speaking is your greatest fear, you might begin with small group discussions, progressing to larger audiences over time. By practicing exposure in controlled, incremental steps, you gradually desensitize yourself to the fear, proving to your mind that these situations are manageable.

Celebrate Small Wins

As you climb each rung, self-reward plays a crucial role in cementing these positive behavior changes. Celebrating progress, no matter how small reinforces your efforts and enhances motivation. Set achievable goals for each step on your ladder and choose meaningful rewards for reaching them. Perhaps after successfully speaking in a meeting, you treat yourself to a favorite activity or indulge in a special meal. These rewards create positive associations with the experience, encouraging further growth. Over time, this cycle of exposure, achievement and reward nurtures a newfound confidence, transforming how you perceive social interactions.

Rewrite Your Script

I invite you to become an active participant in reshaping your social experiences. By understanding the power of thoughts and behaviors, you can rewrite the script of anxiety that has held you back. With practice, patience, and a willingness to face discomfort, you'll be more equipped to engage authentically and confidently.

Overcoming the Fear of Rejection

Every time we step into a room full of strangers or prepare to speak our minds, a familiar knot tightens in our stomachs. It's the fear of rejection, a profoundly ingrained anxiety that whispers caution in our ears. This fear isn't just about the immediate sting of someone turning away; it's rooted in our evolutionary past. Once upon a time, being accepted by our tribe was a matter of survival. Rejection could mean isolation, and isolation spelled danger. Fast forward to today, and our minds still cling to this ancient instinct, even though the stakes have changed. In modern society, rejection rarely threatens our existence, yet it continues to wield enormous influence over our actions and decisions.

Think about this: you're in a meeting, eager to share a new idea. But doubt creeps in, and you stay silent, fearing others might dismiss your thoughts. This scenario is all too common. The fear of rejection can paralyze us, causing us to miss opportunities to connect and grow. However, understanding this fear is the first step toward managing it. Recognizing that it's a natural response can help diminish its power over us.

Cognitive Reframing

To manage rejection fear, several strategies can be incredibly helpful. One technique I find to be extremely effective is cognitive reframing. This involves identifying negative thoughts about rejection and deliberately shifting them to more positive or neutral perspectives. For instance, instead of thinking, "They'll think I'm foolish," you might reframe it as, "This is an opportunity to share my perspective, and it might be valuable."

Vizualisation Techniques

As humans, our imagination creates pictures of every scenario that could unfold. Unfortunately, most of these pictures are negative. The subconscious tries to keep us safe by warning us that unfamiliar territory is ahead. I suggest using conscious visualization techniques to foster positive outcomes and counteract this. Before entering a potentially daunting situation, envision a successful interaction. Picture yourself speaking confidently, see the nods of agreement from those around you, and feel the satisfaction of being heard. This mental rehearsal can prepare you for real-life situations, reducing anxiety and boosting self-assurance.

Embrace Rejection

Embracing rejection itself can be a powerful tool for growth. Many renowned individuals have faced rejection on their paths to success. Consider Steve Jobs, who was once ousted from the very company he founded. His story is a testament that rejection, rather than an end, can be a catalyst for new beginnings. It teaches resilience, sharpens focus, and redirects us toward better opportunities. Lessons learned from rejection are invaluable; they instil humility, encourage adaptability, and can lead to unexpected triumphs.

Lean Into Discomfort

Taking risks in conversation is essential to overcoming the fear of rejection. By stepping out of your comfort zone and initiating challenging dialogues, you build a tolerance for discomfort and learn to navigate it easily. Start by choosing safe environments for practice, like discussion groups or classes where open dialogue is encouraged. Here, you can experiment with expressing your ideas and receiving feedback in a supportive setting. These experiences bolster your confidence and prepare you for more challenging interactions.

In the end, communication is a dance between risk and reward. By understanding the roots of rejection fear and employing strategies to manage it, you can transform potential barriers into building blocks. Embrace the discomfort, take calculated risks, and remember that each conversation is an opportunity to learn and grow. The more you practice, the more adept you will become at turning fear into fuel for connection.

Cultivating a Growth Mindset for Social Success

In your mind's eye, see yourself at a social gathering, surrounded by people effortlessly engaging in lively conversations. You want to join in, but a nagging voice in your head tells you that you're not naturally sociable. This is where the concept of a growth mindset becomes crucial. Coined by psychologist Carol Dweck[3] a growth mindset involves the belief that abilities can be developed through dedication and hard work. It's the opposite of a fixed mindset, which views traits like intelligence and social skills as static. A growth mindset opens doors, allowing us to see setbacks not as failures but as opportunities to learn and improve. In communication, this mindset translates to seeing each interaction as a stepping stone, not a test.

Consider two people at that same gathering. One with a fixed mindset might think, "I'm just not good at small talk," and retreat to a corner. The other, embracing a growth mindset, thinks, "I can get better at this," and seeks out conversation, eager to improve. This mindset shift impacts learning and development significantly. By acknowledging that our abilities aren't set in stone, we free ourselves to experiment, make mistakes and grow. It encourages us to step out of our comfort zones, transforming how we approach communication challenges.

Developing a growth mindset involves specific, actionable strategies. Start by setting achievable communication goals. These could be as simple as initiating one new conversation each day or practicing active listening in meetings. By setting targets, you create an outline for improvement, allowing you to track progress and celebrate small wins.

Befriend Feedback

Embracing feedback is another critical component. Feedback from colleagues or friends provides invaluable insights into your communication style. Use it as a tool for refinement, not a critique of your abilities. Reframe mistakes as learning opportunities rather than failures. When a conversation doesn't go as planned, ask yourself, "What can I learn from this?" This reflection turns each interaction into a chance to grow.

Consistent Practice

Persistence and effort are the backbone of any growth mindset. Consistent practice is vital to enhancing communication skills. A client of mine who was initially terrified of public speaking committed to presenting at a local event every month despite her fear. She signed up to speak at local Probus clubs, Toastmasters, storytelling events, and libraries in her area. Her persistence paid off, and she gradually became a sought-after speaker. Her transformation was a pleasure to watch and highlights the power of effort and the resilience it builds.

The path to improving social skills is not a straight line; it's a series of gradual improvements that compound over time. Each effort, no matter how small, contributes to growth.

3

BUILDING A FOUNDATION OF CONFIDENCE

"Great communication begins with connection." Oprah Winfrey

Years ago, during a workshop, I watched one of the attendees, Paul, struggle to speak up. He sat quietly, his eyes darting between his colleagues as they engaged in animated discussion. Having worked with Paul previously I knew he had brilliant ideas, but his words seemed stuck somewhere between his mind and his mouth.

This struggle is more common than you may think. Regardless of our skills or intellect, many of us have encountered situations where our confidence wavers. We hesitate to speak up, fearing judgment or rejection. This chapter aims to dismantle those barriers, empowering you to find and use your voice.

Confidence in communication is about more than just speaking loudly or often. It's about knowing who you are and expressing that with conviction.

It involves understanding your unique communication style and how it influences your interactions. This self-awareness is the first step in building a solid foundation for confident communication.

Understanding Your Unique Communication Style

Communication styles are diverse and shaped by our personalities, upbringing and experiences. They dictate how we express ourselves and interpret others. Broadly, communication styles fall into four categories: assertive, passive, passive-aggressive and aggressive.

- Assertive communication, the gold standard, involves expressing your thoughts and feelings honestly while respecting others. It promotes healthy interactions and builds trust.

- Passive communicators, on the other hand, often hold back, avoiding conflict at the expense of their own needs. This can lead to misunderstandings and resentment.

- Passive-aggressive style is where individuals express negative emotions indirectly, often leading to confusion and tension.

- Aggressive communicators are confrontational, using anger and dominance, which can create fear and hostility.

Recognizing your communication style is crucial. It helps you understand why you interact the way you do and how others perceive you. To identify your style, consider reflecting on past interactions. Do you often avoid conflict, or do you tend to dominate conversations? Do you express your needs directly, or do you hint at them? To discover your communication style, complete the quiz at the end of this chapter.

Each communication style has its strengths and weaknesses. For example, assertiveness fosters respect and clarity but requires balance to avoid appearing aggressive. Passivity may maintain peace but as said before, often ignores personal needs. Passive-aggressiveness can mask emotions, leading to unresolved conflicts. Aggressiveness might get results but at the cost of relationships. Understanding these dynamics and being open to addressing your weaknesses allows you to leverage your strengths.

For instance, an assertive communicator can enhance their approach by incorporating empathy, ensuring their message is heard and felt.

Flexibility is key, allowing you to navigate different scenarios effectively. You might need to be assertive in negotiations at work but adopt a more passive approach in a supportive role. Sometimes, you may need to blend styles. In some professional settings, assertiveness paired with diplomacy can enhance leadership and teamwork. In personal relationships, balancing assertiveness with compassion can foster deeper connections.

Self-awareness and reflection are the cornerstones of confident communication. They encourage growth and adaptability. Regularly assessing your interactions makes you more attuned to your communication patterns and their impact.

I encourage you to set aside time each week for reflection. Note any significant conversations, your feelings at the time, and any lessons learned. Over time, this practice will produce patterns that help enhance your communication skills and build your confidence to engage fully and authentically in every interaction.

Harnessing the Power of Authenticity

Imagine stepping into a room where every conversation feels like a performance, where each word is carefully crafted to fit an image that isn't yours. We've all been there, feeling the pressure to conform, to say what we think others want to hear. But what if instead of playing a part, you could show up as yourself, genuine and unfiltered?

Authenticity in communication is about being true to who you are, and it's crucial for building meaningful connections. When people sense genuineness, they feel they can trust you, and trust is the foundation of all lasting relationships. It's like opening a window to who you are, inviting others to see the real you rather than just a reflection.

Being authentic also means allowing yourself to be vulnerable. It means admitting that you don't have all the answers or that you're unsure, and that's okay. Vulnerability isn't weakness; it's an invitation for others to engage with you on a deeper level. When you share your struggles or uncertainties, you create space for others to do the same, paving the way for genuine connections. Consider the people you admire most. Often, it's not their successes that resonate with us, but their humanity, their willingness to show their imperfections. This openness encourages others to open up, fostering a sense of community and understanding.

Being authentic breaks down barriers and brings people closer. I know from personal experience. When starting my business many years ago, I was invited to a breakfast meeting with other professional women. We were asked to introduce ourselves one by one; the women before me spoke of their important roles and achievements; they were lawyers, accountants, doctors, and professors. When it was my turn, I didn't want to lie so I told them that I was starting out in my coaching business and I thought I was in the wrong room because I wasn't as successful in my endeavours as the accomplished women who spoke before me. I immediately regretted being so honest and could feel my body shrink back into the chair. But then an incredible thing happened. The next woman to speak said that her business was going into liquidation, and she couldn't sleep at night worrying about it. The woman after her shared that she was trying for a baby and wished she could work part-time and was jealous that my business wasn't taking up my whole life. And so, the stories continued around the table. Each woman taking off her mask, showing their true selves and sharing their struggles. The organizer later told me that in my openness, I had unwittingly given everyone permission to be authentic, and we all benefitted from a more profound connection. To this day, I am still friends with many of the women that were in that room.

Authenticity doesn't mean airing every thought that crosses your mind. It's about sharing the parts of yourself that are true and relevant to the situation. It's a delicate balance. You want to be honest without being rude and open without oversharing. Start by using "I" statements to express your thoughts and feelings. This way, you take ownership of your words, making it clear that you're speaking from your perspective. When you disagree, do so respectfully, acknowledging the other person's viewpoint. It's about being honest while maintaining empathy and respect for others.

Challenges to authenticity abound, especially in a world that often values conformity. Societal norms and expectations can pressure us to hide our true selves. The fear of judgment looms large, making authenticity seem risky. But these challenges can be overcome. Begin by questioning the norms that don't serve you. Ask yourself why you need to conform and whether those expectations align with your values. Strategies for overcoming fear of judgment include surrounding yourself with supportive people and practicing self-compassion. Accept that not everyone will appreciate authenticity, but many will; those are the connections worth fostering.

We can see authentic communication shine through real-world examples. Oprah Winfrey's authenticity has made her a trusted figure worldwide. Her willingness to share personal stories and vulnerabilities has created a profound connection with her audience. Authenticity might mean admitting a mistake at work and proposing a solution rather than brushing it under the rug. Or it could be speaking up about your needs in a relationship, even if it feels uncomfortable. These acts of honesty, though small, have the power to transform interactions from superficial exchanges to meaningful dialogues.

As we explore the power of authenticity, remember that it's not about perfection. It's about showing up as you are, embracing your imperfections and inviting others to do the same. As you can see from my earlier story, authentic communication creates a ripple effect, encouraging those around us to communicate more openly and honestly. It builds trust, deepens relationships and enriches every interaction. As you continue to express yourself authentically, you'll find that your connections become more genuine, your conversations more rewarding and your interactions more fulfilling. Each step toward authenticity is a step toward more profound, meaningful communication.

Building a Supportive Social Environment

Creating a supportive network is very important in building social confidence. Imagine stepping into a space where people understand your challenges and where sharing your experiences feels natural. Having friends or groups who share similar struggles can significantly alleviate the weight of social anxiety. It's about finding those who resonate with your journey, those who nod knowingly when you express your fears.

Engaging with supportive online communities or forums can also be a lifeline. These digital spaces offer anonymity and a platform to connect with others facing similar issues. Here, you can exchange stories, offer advice, and celebrate small victories without fearing judgment. In these interactions, you realize you're not alone; a whole world of people is navigating similar paths, ready to offer a listening ear and a compassionate heart.

Cultivating positive social connections requires intentionality and openness. It's about seeking out environments that feel safe and nurturing, where interactions are genuine and supportive. Initiating conversations with like-minded individuals can form the bedrock of such connections. Start by attending events or joining groups that align with your interests. Whether it's a book club, a sports team, or an art class, shared passions often pave the way for deeper connections. These activities provide a natural context for conversation, reducing the pressure to perform or impress. As you engage, focus on building relationships that are nurturing, where you can be yourself without fear of judgment. Approach these interactions with kindness and authenticity, allowing them to unfold naturally.

Communication plays a vital role in expressing your needs and boundaries within these relationships. It's about asserting yourself respectfully and ensuring your comfort and well-being are prioritized. This might mean saying no to invitations that feel overwhelming or asking for support when you need it. Learning to express your feelings openly can strengthen your connections, as it encourages honesty and transparency. When you articulate your needs, you give others the opportunity to understand and support you. This exchange fosters trust and mutual respect, creating a foundation where both parties feel valued and heard. Practicing these communication skills can transform your interactions, making them more fulfilling and less anxiety-inducing.

Building a personalized support system involves identifying reliable and empathetic individuals who can offer encouragement and accountability. These are the people who will check in with you, celebrate your successes, and lend a shoulder when times get tough. Consider creating a regular schedule to connect with them through phone calls, texts, or in-person meetings. These check-ins provide a consistent source of support, helping you stay grounded and motivated. Share your goals with them and invite their feedback and encouragement. A network like this bolsters your confidence and reminds you that you're part of something larger than yourself. It's a reminder that even when anxiety feels insurmountable, you're never alone.

As you navigate building this network, remember it's an evolving process. Relationships take time to develop, and it's okay to start small. Trust grows with each interaction, blossoming into a network of support that empowers you to face challenges head-on. Surrounding yourself with understanding individuals can be transformative, turning anxiety from an isolating experience into one of shared understanding and camaraderie.

Quiz : Discover Your Communication Style

Instructions: Answer each question honestly. Choose the option that most closely aligns with how you usually respond in the situations described.

When someone interrupts you while you're speaking, how do you typically react?

A. I stop talking and let them speak.

B. I express my frustration either then or later in an indirect way.

C. I point out the interruption and ask to finish what I was saying.

D. I might snap at them or interrupt them back.

How do you handle criticism from others?

A. I tend to stay quiet even if I disagree.

B. I say nothing but later complain about it to someone else.

C. I listen, ask questions, and try to use the feedback constructively.

D. I often feel attacked and respond defensively.

What is. your approach to expressing disagreement?

A. I rarely express disagreement to avoid conflict.

B. I might not say anything but will show my displeasure in other ways.

C. I clearly state why I disagree in a respectful manner.

D. I am very direct and can get loud or demanding.

In a group decision-making process, how do you contribute?

A. I tend to go along with what others decide.

B. I might not voice my opinion and possibly resent the decision later.

C. I share my opinions and consider others' points of view as well.

D. I push hard for my ideas and struggle to accept other perspectives.

How do you feel about asking others for help?

A. I hesitate to ask for help as I don't want to bother others.

B. I complain about my situation hoping someone will offer to help.

C. I comfortably ask for help when needed and offer help in return.

D. I demand help from others and might get impatient.

When you're angry about something, how do you express it?

A. I keep it to myself to avoid confrontation.

B. I might not say anything directly but will make sarcastic comments.

C. I calmly explain why I'm upset and discuss possible solutions.

D. I often let others know exactly why I'm angry in a heated manner.

What do you do if you need something from someone who is busy?

A. I wait until they are free, even if it takes a long time.

B. I wait. I might make passive comments about how busy they always are.

C. I ask them when would be a good time to talk or help.

D. I insist they make time for me as soon as possible.

How do you respond when you feel you're being treated unfairly?

A. I often don't speak up to avoid making things worse.

B. I may not confront the issue directly but hold a grudge.

C. I address the issue directly and seek a fair resolution.

D. I get angry and demand an explanation.

What's your usual way of handling a conflict with a friend?

A. I try to smooth things over, sometimes ignoring my own feelings.

B. I give them the silent treatment until they figure out what's wrong.

C. I discuss the problem openly and seek a mutual understanding.

D. I confront them aggressively to make my point.

How do you express appreciation or gratitude to someone?

A. I feel it, but don't always say it directly.

B. I might send a message later instead of saying it in person.

C. I openly express my gratitude and appreciation.

D. I might not say thanks unless it's a big favor.

How do you deal with being given tasks you feel are beneath you?

A. I do them quietly without complaint.

B. I might do them but not without expressing some sarcasm.

C. I discuss the assignment with the person to understand their rationale.

D. I refuse or argue about the appropriateness of the tasks.

When someone shares good news, how do you respond?

A. I might smile, but I'm quiet.

B. I say congratulations, but I might not seem enthusiastic.

C. I respond enthusiastically and encourage them to tell me more.

D. I might make a quick comment, then switch the conversation to my experiences.

Scoring Guide:

Mostly A's: Passive Communication Style

Mostly B's: Passive-Aggressive Communication Style

Mostly C's: Assertive Communication Style

Mostly D's: Aggressive Communication Style

A: Passive Communication Style

Strengths:

Good at listening and avoiding conflicts.

Often perceived as easy-going and approachable.

Weaknesses:

May not express personal needs or opinions, leading to potential misunderstanding and resentment.

Can be overlooked in personal and professional settings due to a lack of assertiveness.

Improvement Tips:

Practice stating your needs and opinions in small, non-threatening settings to build confidence.

Work on setting and respecting personal boundaries. Remember, it's okay to say no.

Enhance your self-esteem through affirmations and positive self-talk to support more assertive behavior.

B: Passive-Aggressive Communication Style

Strengths:

Can be highly diplomatic, managing to navigate through difficult situations subtly.

Often creative in expressing feelings without direct confrontation.

Weaknesses:

Indirect communication can lead to misunderstandings and unresolved conflicts.

May harbor resentment and cause others to feel frustrated when the real feelings are masked by sarcasm or backhanded comments.

Improvement Tips:

Aim for direct communication about your feelings and needs. Be honest and open to prevent misunderstandings.

Reflect on the reasons behind your indirectness; understanding these can help you address issues more directly.

Learn to manage anger and frustration through healthier outlets like exercise, journaling, or speaking with a therapist.

C: Assertive Communication Style

Strengths:

Generally clear, direct, and respected for honest communication.

Good at negotiating and expressing needs without infringing on the rights of others.

Weaknesses:

May sometimes come off as too blunt or straightforward, which can be perceived as insensitivity.

Risk of overconfidence which might lead to less compromise.

Improvement Tips:

Focus on maintaining empathy and consider others' emotions when you communicate.

Practice active listening to ensure that you understand others' perspectives and needs as well.

Continue to practice self-awareness to ensure that assertiveness does not slip into aggressiveness.

D: Aggressive Communication Style

Strengths:

Very clear about personal wants and needs.

Can be highly effective in leadership roles where decision-making and direction are required.

Weaknesses:

Often seen as overbearing, which can alienate others and create hostility.

Might overlook others' needs, leading to poor relationships and team dynamics.

Improvement Tips:

Work on emotional regulation skills to handle conflicts calmly and without aggression.

Practice active listening to understand and validate others' points of view.

Focus on collaborative problem-solving techniques to ensure all voices are heard and integrated into decisions.

By identifying your primary communication style, you can leverage your strengths and actively work on your weaknesses to improve your overall effectiveness in both personal and professional interactions.

Are you ready to master small talk? You will be once you realise how valuable it is? Turn the page because that's what we're discussing in the next chapter.

4

MASTERING SMALL TALK

"Small talk, though often dismissed as trivial, serves a vital purpose."
Anne McKeown

Picture yourself at an after-work networking event. Mingling voices surround you. You're holding a drink, glancing around and you notice a familiar feeling creeping in—a mix of excitement and anxiety. You want to connect, to join in, but the right words seem out of reach. We've all been there, standing at the threshold of interaction, where small talk acts as the bridge.

This chapter is about perfecting the art of starting conversations, turning that initial awkwardness into ease. Small talk, though often dismissed as trivial, serves a vital purpose. It sets the stage, breaking down barriers and laying the groundwork for deeper connections. Effective icebreakers are the key to this process. They open doors, inviting others into conversation with warmth and curiosity.

Icebreakers are more than just a tool; they're a way to transform the social environment. When used effectively, they ease tension and invite genuine engagement. They help you move past the initial stiffness, setting a tone that encourages openness. Icebreakers can dissolve the invisible walls that separate us, whether at a networking event, a casual gathering, or a business meeting. They are the first step in building rapport, signaling you're approachable and interested. The right icebreaker can turn a room full of strangers into a group of potential connections within minutes.

At networking events full of professionals from all walks of life, I've asked,"What brings you here today?" It's perfect for this situation. It's open-ended, inviting the other person to share their motivations and interests, creating a natural segue into a more detailed conversation. In a more casual setting, like a party, I've asked, "Have you tried the [food/drink]? What do you think of it?" This approach is light and engaging and taps into the shared experience of the event itself. Or perhaps you're catching up with someone you haven't seen lately. "What's been the highlight of your week so far?" is a question that opens the door to personal stories and shows genuine interest in their life.

Building a toolkit of versatile icebreakers is like having a Swiss Army knife for social situations. These questions and statements are adaptable, suitable for different contexts, and can be tailored to reflect your personality. They serve as reliable starting points while allowing flexibility to adjust based on the setting and the person you're speaking with. The goal is to engage without overwhelming and to pique curiosity without prying. A well-chosen icebreaker can be the difference between a fleeting exchange and a memorable connection.

As you engage, it's crucial to read the room—literally. Pay attention to body language and facial expressions, as they can reveal more than words. Are they leaning in, making eye contact, or smiling? These are signs of interest and receptiveness. Conversely, crossed arms, glances around the room, or monosyllabic answers might indicate discomfort or disinterest. Listening for verbal cues and tone of voice also provides insight. Are their responses enthusiastic or hesitant? Do they mirror your energy, or are they holding back? Adjust your approach by shifting topics or asking more open-ended questions to encourage participation.

Creativity and personalization are your allies in crafting unique icebreakers. Let your personality shine through, using humor or shared interests to make the conversation yours. If you share a love for a particular hobby or current event, weave it into your opening line. Humor, when used mindfully, can break the tension and invite laughter, a universal connector. A well-timed joke or witty observation can disarm and delight, making the interaction memorable. However, it's important to gauge the appropriateness of humor, ensuring it aligns with the setting and the individual's comfort level. This blend of creativity and personalization not only differentiates your approach but also enhances the authenticity of the exchange.

Craft Your Own Icebreakers

Take a moment to jot down three icebreakers that resonate with you. Consider your interests, recent experiences, or current events that intrigue you. How can these be molded into engaging opening lines? Reflect on past interactions—what worked well, and what fell flat? Use these insights to refine your approach, creating a personal repertoire of icebreakers that feel natural and inviting. As you practice, notice how these openers influence the flow of conversation and the connections you form.

Transforming Small Talk into Meaningful Dialogue

Small talk can often feel shallow, a necessary but mundane start to conversations. Yet, the beauty of small talk lies in its potential, a stepping stone toward more profound, more meaningful dialogue. It's an opportunity to transition from surface-level chatter to conversations that leave you feeling enriched and connected.

Active listening is key to this transition, an often-underestimated skill that transforms interactions. By truly listening, you catch nuances and unspoken cues hinting at someone's passions or interests. Follow-up questions play a vital role too. They show you're engaged and willing to explore beyond the initial topic. When someone mentions their recent vacation, don't just nod. Ask about their favorite moment or why they chose that destination. These questions invite elaboration, nudging the dialogue into more substantive territory.

Transitioning to deeper discussions requires an eye for opportunities. Spotting these moments is like reading between the lines. A casual mention of a hobby might be an invitation to delve into a shared passion. Recognizing these cues, you can smoothly guide the conversation to topics that resonate more deeply. This requires a blend of curiosity and intuition, allowing the conversation to evolve naturally. Steer discussions toward meaningful subjects using open-ended questions. These questions can't be answered with a simple yes or no, encouraging others to share more. Instead of asking, "Do you like your job?" try, "What do you find most rewarding about your work?" This invites the other person to reflect and reveal more, setting the stage for a richer dialogue. Sharing personal insights or anecdotes also deepens the conversation. By offering a glimpse into your own experiences, you create a space where others feel comfortable doing the same. It's about creating a dialogue that is reciprocal and genuine.

Empathy and curiosity are your allies in this endeavor. They fuel your interest in others, allowing you to see things from their perspective. Empathy involves more than just understanding; it's about conveying that understanding in your responses. Instead of a generic "I see," try something like,"That sounds challenging, how did you manage it?" This acknowledges their experience and encourages them to open up further. Curiosity drives you to ask questions that matter, ones that reveal stories and insights. It's about showing genuine interest and a desire to learn and connect. Encouraging others to share their stories is crucial. Often, people hold back, unsure if their experiences are worth sharing. By expressing curiosity, you signal that you're not just listening but eager to understand their world.

Consider a networking event where you're speaking with a colleague about a recent industry conference. Instead of sticking to the basics, you ask, "What was the most surprising thing you learned there?" This question transitions the conversation from mere information exchange to a discussion about insights and learning. The colleague shares an innovative idea they encountered, sparking a dialogue about industry trends and personal growth.

Think about a casual chat with a neighbor. They mention their garden, and instead of just commenting on the weather, you ask about what they enjoy growing the most. This leads to a conversation about sustainable living and personal values, topics that might not have surfaced otherwise.

These examples illustrate the power of transitioning small talk into meaningful dialogue. They show how simple questions can uncover layers of experience and understanding. The conversations we cherish are often those where we feel heard and valued, where the exchange moves beyond the mundane. Small talk is the gateway, but the empathy, curiosity and willingness to explore deeper turn ordinary exchanges into significant connections.

Finding Common Ground

Imagine you're at a friend's dinner party, surrounded by unfamiliar faces. The conversation ebbs and flows around you, and you search for a way to connect with the person beside you. In such moments, discovering common ground becomes a lifeline. It transforms strangers into acquaintances and acquaintances into friends. Shared interests serve as the glue that binds us, turning fleeting exchanges into meaningful connections. When you identify a mutual hobby, a recent news event, or even a shared acquaintance, you create a bridge that spans the gap between you and the other person. This connection fosters rapport and lays the foundation for deeper engagement, making the conversation feel less like an obligation and more like a shared adventure.

Topics with universal appeal offer a reliable starting point. Travel, for example, is a rich vein to mine. Whether it's the destinations you've visited, dream of seeing, or simply the allure of exploring new places, travel stories are laden with vivid imagery and personal insight. Discussing recent books or movies can also ignite a spark. Narratives often reflect our values and experiences, providing a canvas for dialogue. "Have you read anything interesting lately?" or "What movie has caught your attention?" are questions that invite others to share their tastes and opinions.

Food, too, is a universal connector. Given our shared love for culinary delights, conversations about favorite meals, new recipes, or memorable dining experiences will likely resonate with almost anyone.

Uncovering commonalities is an art, one that involves curiosity and a dash of storytelling. As you engage, ask open-ended questions that invite others to share their experiences. "What inspired your love for travel?" or "How did that book change your perspective?" are inquiries that encourage others to open up. Sharing your own stories in response creates a reciprocal and engaging dialogue. This exchange of narratives not only highlights similarities but also builds a sense of camaraderie.

Humor can be particularly effective in uncovering common ground. Light-hearted jokes about shared experiences or playful banter about everyday mishaps can make the atmosphere more relaxed and enjoyable.

Navigating conversations requires an awareness of potential pitfalls. Certain topics, like politics or religion, can be divisive, especially in initial interactions. Such subjects often evoke strong opinions and emotions, risking conflict in an otherwise pleasant exchange. It's wise to steer clear until you know the other person better and feel confident that the conversation can remain respectful and balanced. Similarly, overly personal questions can intrude upon privacy, making others uncomfortable. Striking the right balance involves gauging the other person's openness and comfort level, ensuring that your questions invite rather than intrude.

Finding common ground is a delicate balance of curiosity and empathy.

It requires an openness to explore new perspectives and a willingness to share your own. As you navigate these conversations, remember that the goal is not to agree on everything but to find those precious moments of connection that make the dialogue worthwhile. By focusing on shared interests and avoiding contentious topics, you create a space where genuine rapport can flourish, transforming simple exchanges into enriching experiences.

Navigating Awkward Silences with Confidence

There you are, mid-conversation, when suddenly the words dry up, leaving a silence hanging between you and the other person. It's a moment we've all experienced, one that can make your heart race and your mind scramble for the nearest exit. But what if these pauses aren't the conversational villains, we often make them out to be? Silences in conversation can serve as valuable moments of reflection or transition, offering a break for both parties to process what's been said. They provide the opportunity to gather thoughts and consider the next direction the conversation might take. Instead of viewing these silences as uncomfortable voids to be quickly filled, recognize them as natural pauses that are part of any dialogue.

Managing pauses with ease involves a mix of humor, observation, and a touch of creativity. When the silence stretches, sometimes a light-hearted comment can ease the tension, inviting a shared laugh and shifting the focus away from the awkwardness. You might comment on something amusing in your surroundings, like the quirky art on the wall or the peculiar choice of music. This not only fills the silence but can also redirect the conversation towards a new topic. Alternatively, use the silence as a moment to make an external observation. Perhaps you notice a beautiful sunset outside or the bustling energy of the café. These observations can inspire a fresh angle for the conversation, guiding it naturally into new territory without forcing the flow.

Patience and composure are your allies during these moments. Staying relaxed and present allows the conversation to evolve at its own pace, without the pressure to rush or force words. As mentioned previously, simple breathing exercises can help maintain calm. Try inhaling deeply through your nose, holding for a moment, and then exhaling slowly and quietly. This practice calms your nerves and enables you to stay grounded in the moment. Focusing on the other person's non-verbal cues, can also keep you engaged without feeling the need to fill every pause with words. By embracing the silence, you demonstrate confidence and comfort in the conversation, allowing both parties the space to think and reflect.

I've found that silences have punctuated some of my most memorable conversations. There was a time I sat across from a friend at a café, where a sudden pause led us both to gaze out the window. The shared silence was filled with an unspoken understanding, and when we resumed talking, it was about something entirely different—deeper, more personal. That pause had allowed our thoughts to wander and reconnect on a new level. Another incident was during a recent family gathering where a lull in the conversation allowed my aunt to share a story we hadn't heard before, the content of which brought us all closer.

Remember that silences are not your enemy. They can be moments of introspection and opportunities for new beginnings. Embrace them with patience, use them to your advantage, and let them guide you to connections that resonate. Silences needn't be feared; they can bridge understanding and depth. As we move forward, consider how pauses can enhance your interactions, offering clarity and insight. Each pause is a chance for a new beginning, a fresh perspective, or a deeper connection.

Social ice-breakers to help you start a conversation.

"Have you read any good books lately?"
This can be a gateway to talking about common interests in literature or recommendations.

"What's the best movie you've seen recently?"
Movies are a popular topic and can lead to longer, engaging conversations.

"Are you a cat person or a dog person?"
This question is light-hearted and can lead to funny stories about pets.

"What's your favorite travel destination?"
Travel elicits memories of good times and dreams of future adventures."

"Do you have a favorite local restaurant or coffee shop?"
Recommendations for food or hangouts often lead to mutual interests or plans to visit them together.

"What kind of music do you like to listen to?"
Music is a universal language and discussing favorite genres or artists can be very bonding.

"Have you picked up any new hobbies recently?"
This can uncover new activities they are passionate about or challenges they've taken on.

"What's the best piece of advice you've ever received?"
This question can lead to meaningful conversations about life lessons and personal philosophies.

"If you could learn one new professional or personal skill, what would it be?"
This opens up a conversation about aspirations and interests.

"What's your go-to comfort food?"
Food often connects people and talking about comfort foods can be a warm and friendly topic.

Professional ice-breakers to help you facilitate conversation in a workplace or networking environment.

"How did you start your career in this industry?"
Understanding someone's professional journey can offer insights and shared experiences.

"Have you attended any interesting webinars or conferences lately?"
Sharing knowledge gained from industry events can foster learning and partnership opportunities.

"What trends do you see shaping our industry?"
Discussing future predictions can show their insight into industry dynamics and their forward-thinking mindset.

"What do you enjoy most about working in this field?"
This can highlight the positives of the industry and what motivates them professionally.

"What's the last professional book you read and would recommend?"
Recommendations can lead to shared learning resources and further discussion on professional growth.

"What project are you currently excited about at work?"
This question directly relates to their professional interests and can spark a conversation about shared areas of expertise or different fields.

"Who in your field do you most admire and why?"
This can lead to discussions about industry leaders, inspirational figures, and the qualities valued in your shared profession.

"What's one piece of technology you can't work without?"
Discussing tools of the trade can lead to practical tips and mutual interests in tech.

"What professional achievement are you most proud of?"
This allows them to share successes, which can be inspirational and enlightening.

"What's the best career advice you've ever received?"
Sharing and receiving advice can build a foundation for a mentorship-like relationship.

5

DE-CODING NON-VERBAL COMMUNICATION

"You can't not communicate. Everything you say and do sends a message."
James Borg

Imagine you're at a friend's birthday party, trying to converse with someone new. The words come easily, but something feels off. You can't quite put your finger on it, yet an invisible barrier seems to linger. This is the silent interplay of body language—an unspoken dialogue that shapes our interactions profoundly. While we often focus on what we say, how we say it can be just as important, if not more so.

The 7-38-55 Rule

Dr. Albert Mehrabian, a researcher and professor emeritus of psychology at UCLA, studied human communication patterns in the 1960s. His research[4] specifically focused on inconsistent messages involving feelings and attitudes. He concluded that the interpretation of a message is 7 percent verbal (words only), 38 percent vocal (tone of voice, inflection, and other sounds), and 55 percent non-verbal (body language, facial expressions, posture, etc.). This breakdown is commonly summarized as the "7-38-55 Rule." It's important to note that this statistic applies primarily to situations where someone communicates feelings or attitudes; it isn't a general rule that applies to all types of communication. Having said that, it is a statistic we can't ignore. Understanding non-verbal communication allows you to read between the lines, offering insights into emotions and intentions that might otherwise remain hidden.

Body Language Basics

Body language basics begin with posture and stance, foundational elements conveying openness or defensiveness. An open posture, characterized by uncrossed arms and a relaxed stance, signals receptivity and ease. It invites others in, creating an atmosphere of approachability. Conversely, crossed arms or a rigid posture can suggest defensiveness or discomfort, erecting an invisible wall between you and the other person. This is not just about physical positioning; it's about the emotional message you project.

Our gestures also play a crucial role in communication. They can emphasize spoken words, adding clarity and passion, or contradict them, leading to confusion. For instance, a nod while saying "yes" reinforces agreement, while a shrug might suggest uncertainty, even if you are verbally saying "yes".

Observing body language cues requires attention to detail and context. Signs of interest or disengagement can be subtle yet telling. Leaning in, maintaining eye contact, and nodding are indicators of engagement and interest. They show that the person is present and actively participating in the exchange. On the other hand, glancing around the room, fidgeting, or checking a phone can signal disengagement, suggesting that their mind is elsewhere. Stress or discomfort often manifests through physical cues such as clenched fists, tense shoulders, or rapid blinking. These signs reveal underlying emotions that words might not explicitly express. You gain a deeper understanding of the emotional landscape within interactions by tuning into these cues.

Practical Applications

Your body language can significantly influence the outcomes of any meeting or discussion. Consider the two following examples:

Workplace Interaction:
In a team meeting, a manager is discussing the rollout of a new project. Sarah, a team member, has concerns about the timeline, believing it to be too aggressive. During the meeting, Sarah sits with her arms crossed, leaning slightly back in her chair, and avoids eye contact with her manager. Her facial expressions are flat with occasional frowns.

Influence of Body Language:
Sarah's body language signals disapproval and disengagement. The manager, picking up on these cues, might perceive Sarah as resistant or uncooperative. This could lead the manager to dismiss her concerns without fully understanding them, potentially missing out on valuable feedback that could improve the project's success. Conversely, if Sarah maintained open body language—leaning forward, nodding, and maintaining eye contact—it might encourage a more constructive conversation and willingness from the manager to consider her feedback.

Negotiation Interaction:
Alex is negotiating a contract with a potential new client. The stakes are high, and Alex wants to secure a profitable and fair deal. Throughout the negotiation he uses open palm gestures, maintains good eye contact and nods when the client speaks, signaling attentiveness and openness. When discussing terms, Alex's posture is upright but relaxed, and he uses his hands to emphasize key points gently.

Influence of Body Language:
Alex's body language conveys confidence and sincerity, making the client feel respected and valued. This approach fosters a positive atmosphere and encourages the client to be more open and transparent about what they need from the deal. As a result, both parties are more likely to find a mutually beneficial agreement.

These examples illustrate how subtle non-verbal cues can significantly affect the dynamics and outcomes of professional interactions.

Learning From Experts – Oprah Winfrey's Interview Techniques

Oprah Winfrey, renowned for her empathetic and effective interview style, employs body language to connect deeply with her guests. She often leans forward slightly, signaling interest and engagement. Her facial expressions mirror those of her guest, which helps to establish a rapport and shows empathy. For instance, during a poignant interview with Lance Armstrong, Oprah's use of nodding and maintaining consistent eye contact encouraged him to open up about his use of performance-enhancing drugs—a topic he had long denied publicly.

Oprah's body language sends a powerful message of trust and sincerity to her interviewees, often leading them to share more freely and deeply than they might in a more conventional interview setting. This technique not only enhances the quality of information received but also deeply engages the audience, making her interviews memorable and impactful.

This example highlights how non-verbal cues can be strategically used to enhance verbal communication. It shows that good interviewers do more than just ask questions; they communicate through their posture, expressions, and gestures to create an environment where open and honest dialogue can flourish.

Context is Key

Context is key when interpreting body language. The same gesture can carry different meanings depending on the setting. In a casual environment, slouching might indicate relaxation, while in a formal setting, it could be seen as disrespect or lack of interest.

Environmental factors also shape physical expression. A crowded room, for instance, might lead to more constrained body movements, whereas an open space might encourage expansive gestures. Understanding the nuances of context allows you to interpret body language more accurately, avoiding misinterpretations that could lead to misunderstandings.

People Watching

Practice is essential to develop your reading body language skills. People-watching can be fun and valuable, offering a real-world classroom where you can observe interactions and note various cues. Visit a park, café, or mall, and watch how people communicate without words. How do they express interest or boredom? What physical signals accompany their emotions? I've created a guide for you to follow at the end of this chapter.

You could also try analyzing body language in films or TV shows. These visual mediums provide rich examples of non-verbal communication, allowing you to pause, reflect, and dissect interactions in detail. Observing fictional characters can hone your ability to recognize body language signals in your own life.

The Subtleties of Facial Expressions

Imagine sitting across from someone, conversing, when their face subtly shifts. Perhaps it's the flicker of a smile or the brief furrow of a brow. These fleeting moments, often overlooked, hold immense power in revealing emotions and intentions.

Facial expressions are a universal language that transcends words, offering insights into the emotional undercurrents of our interactions. Even when words fail or deceive, expressions like happiness, sadness, and anger speak clearly and honestly. These basic expressions are recognized worldwide, serving as a shared human vocabulary. However, the human face is also capable of complexity, expressing mixed emotions that can convey nuanced feelings.

Understanding these facial nuances requires a keen eye and a willingness to look beyond the obvious. Micro-expressions, for instance, are brief, involuntary facial movements that occur in less than a second. They offer a glimpse into a person's true emotions, often before they have time to mask them. Recognizing these micro-expressions involves paying attention to quick changes in facial muscles, such as fleeting lips tightening.

Eye contact is another critical element. It can signal interest, confidence, or challenge, while avoidance might suggest discomfort or deceit. Observing these eye movement shifts and subtle changes in eyebrow positioning can reveal much about a person's emotional state.

Emotional congruence is at the heart of effective communication. When facial expressions align with spoken words, they create a harmony that feels authentic and trustworthy.

However, discrepancies between words and expressions can signal deception or hidden feelings. Imagine someone saying, "I'm fine," while their eyes dart away and their mouth tightens; such mismatches alert us to underlying emotions that contradict the verbal message. Conversely, when verbal and facial cues are consistent, they enhance the message, reinforcing sincerity and openness. Recognizing these cues helps us navigate conversations with greater empathy and understanding, allowing us to respond appropriately to the unspoken feelings of others.

Train Your Brain to Read Facial Expressions

Improving your ability to read facial expressions is a skill that can be cultivated through practice. One effective method is using flashcards with different facial expressions. By repeatedly identifying the emotions depicted, you train your brain to notice subtle differences and improve your recognition skills.

There are some great interactive apps available that offer training in recognizing micro-expressions, providing real-time feedback as you practice. I've played around with these two:

Face Reader - this software is often used in academic and professional research settings.

Humintell Mix – this app was developed by a team of psychologists and offers a mix of training on micro-expressions, body language, and lie detection.

Engaging with tools like these regularly will enhance your sensitivity to the emotional states of those around you, enabling you to connect more deeply and authentically. Each smile, frown, and glance tell a story, and with practice, you'll become adept at reading the narratives written across the faces of those you encounter.

Understanding Cultural Nuances in Non-Verbal Cues

Stepping into a new culture can feel like walking into a room where everyone speaks a different language, yet no one utters a word. Non-verbal communication is woven with gestures, expressions and spatial dynamics that vary significantly across cultural contexts.

In some cultures, personal space is almost sacred, with invisible boundaries that dictate comfort levels. Stand too close, and you might inadvertently step into someone's bubble, causing discomfort. In others, close proximity might signify warmth and friendship, an invitation to closeness. Understanding these differences is crucial, as missteps can easily lead to awkwardness or offense.

Gestures, too, carry a spectrum of meanings. A simple thumbs up, which might be seen as a positive affirmation in one culture, could be interpreted differently in another, perhaps even as an insult. Each gesture carries a history, a cultural context that shapes its interpretation.

Navigating these cultural differences requires a combination of research and mindfulness. We delve deeper into this topic in chapter ten.

Using Your Own Body Language to Build Rapport

You can foster trust and build rapport with others by consciously using body language. One effective technique is mirroring, subtly reflecting the other person's posture and movements. This isn't about mimicry; it's about creating a rhythm that resonates with the person you're interacting with. When done naturally, it signals alignment and understanding, making others feel more comfortable and valued.

Open gestures play a crucial role in appearing welcoming and approachable. Think of gestures as the punctuation marks of non-verbal communication. They add emphasis and clarity to your message. Open palm gestures, for instance, suggest honesty and inviting others into the conversation. Avoiding closed-off gestures, like crossing your arms or turning your body away, can prevent the creation of barriers. Instead, face the person fully and use expansive and inclusive gestures. This openness is a non-verbal invitation to engage, signaling you're present and interested in the interaction.

Maintaining positive body language throughout a conversation enhances your presence and impact. Eye contact is a powerful tool here. It demonstrates engagement, showing the other person you're attentive and invested in their words. However, it's important to balance eye contact to feel natural, avoiding an intense stare that might appear intimidating.

Alongside eye contact, controlling nervous habits is vital. Fidgeting, tapping your foot, or playing with your hair can distract from the conversation and convey anxiety. Knowing these habits allows you to manage them, reinforcing a calm and confident demeanor.

To refine your skills in using body language, practice through role-playing scenarios. This exercise allows you to test different approaches and receive feedback on your perceived non-verbal cues.

You might play the role of a leader in a meeting or engage in a casual conversation with a friend, experimenting with various gestures and postures. Recording these interactions and reviewing them offers valuable insights. It allows you to see yourself from an outside perspective, highlighting areas for improvement and reinforcing effective techniques. By practicing regularly, you'll build a repertoire of non-verbal skills that enhance your communication in diverse situations.

Body Language in Leadership

In leadership, body language becomes a foundation of influence and authority. Effective leaders use authoritative gestures to assert confidence and command respect. These gestures include standing tall, using deliberate movements, and occupying space confidently.

Amy Cuddy, social psychologist and author of "Presence," says, "Our bodies change our minds, and our minds can change our behavior, and our behavior can change our outcomes. In her book she discusses how adopting powerful, expansive poses can increase feelings of confidence and can impact our chances of success—a concept she calls "power posing."

Most successful leaders know how to balance this authority with approachability. They combine assertive gestures with warmth, using open postures and genuine smiles to convey strength and empathy. This blend of qualities fosters trust and inspires those around them, creating an environment where people feel guided and supported.

Step-by-Step Guide to Body Language Observation

Step 1: Select the Right Location

Choose a public place where people frequently interact, such as a park, cafe or shopping mall. Ensure the location provides a good vantage point from which to observe without intruding on privacy.

Step 2: Prepare for Observation

Bring a notebook and pen to record your observations or use a digital device.
Settle yourself where you can watch without being noticed, as natural behavior is more likely when people don't feel watched.

Step 3: Decide on Focus Areas

Before you begin, decide what specific aspects of body language you want to focus on. This could be gestures, facial expressions, postures, or interpersonal distances.
You can start with one focus area and gradually add more as you become more experienced and comfortable with observation.

Step 4: Observe and Record

Spend at least 30 minutes observing people. Note down key behaviors.

Gestures:
Are they expansive or restricted?
Do they seem to match the verbal communication?

Posture:
Is it open or closed?
How does it change in different interactions?

Facial Expressions:
What emotions are being displayed?
How do these relate to the conversation?

Eye Contact:
Is it direct or avoidant?
What might this indicate about the person's comfort level or interest?

Try to see if there's a pattern or trigger that changes a person's body language.

Step 5: Analyze Context

Reflect on how the context might influence the body language you observed. Consider factors like the setting, the number of people and the apparent relationships between individuals.

Step 6: Reflect on Your Observations

After your observation session, spend some time reflecting on what you noted. Ask yourself:
What surprised you?
Were there any interactions that were particularly informative?
How did the context appear to affect people's behavior?

Step 7: Apply What You Learned

Think about how you can apply your newfound insights into body language in your daily interactions.
Practice being more mindful of your own non-verbal cues and how they could be perceived.

Step 8: Repeat and Expand

Regular practice will enhance your observational skills. Repeat this exercise in different settings to broaden your understanding.

As you become more skilled, try to observe more subtle aspects of non-verbal communication, such as micro-expressions or the synchronization of movements between people in conversation.

By following these steps, you will develop a deeper understanding of body language and its impact on communication.

6

EMPATHY AND ACTIVE LISTENING

"Empathy is seeing with the eyes of another; listening with the ears of another and feeling with the heart of another." Alfred Adler

The room is filled with laughter and chatter at a family gathering, and you notice your cousin sitting quietly in the corner. Something inside you shifts as you approach, sensing the weight of words unsaid.

This instinctive pull towards understanding is empathy—a profound yet often misunderstood component of human connection. Empathy transcends mere sympathy; it is the ability to step into another's shoes and perceive the world through their eyes. It is the cornerstone of effective communication, bridging the gap between individuals and fostering a sense of shared humanity. Empathy transforms superficial interactions into meaningful dialogues that resonate long after the conversation ends. It's not just about understanding others; it's about being understood.

Empathy plays a pivotal role in building relationships, acting as a catalyst for trust and rapport. Consider a friend confiding in you about a recent struggle. An empathetic response would involve listening intently, acknowledging their feelings, and offering support without judgment. This approach contrasts sharply with a non-empathetic reaction, where the focus shifts to offering unsolicited advice or dismissing their emotions as trivial. When empathy is present, it fosters an environment where individuals feel valued and heard, laying the groundwork for more resilient relationships.

The impact of empathy extends beyond personal connections, influencing professional interactions as well. Empathy can enhance collaboration and understanding in the workplace, allowing teams to function more effectively and with greater cohesion. When colleagues feel understood, it fosters an atmosphere of trust, encouraging open communication and sharing ideas.

Developing Empathy

Developing empathy requires intentional practice, and the rewards are immeasurable. One effective strategy, known as perspective-taking, is the exercise of stepping into someone else's shoes. This involves setting aside personal biases and judgments to fully embrace another person's experience. It requires an open mind and the willingness to see beyond your own viewpoint.

Another powerful tool for cultivating empathy is reflective listening. By actively listening and reflecting back what you've heard, you signal understanding and validation. This practice deepens the conversation and strengthens your connection with the speaker. For example, saying, "It sounds like you're feeling frustrated because of the deadline," shows empathy by acknowledging the other person's emotional state and helps clarify their message.

Role-playing scenarios can further enhance empathy by allowing you to experience diverse perspectives firsthand. These exercises increase awareness of others' emotions and experiences, fostering a more empathetic approach to communication.

Despite its importance, maintaining empathy can be challenging, especially when personal biases or emotional fatigue intervene. Barriers like these can cloud our judgment and limit our ability to connect.

Overcoming these obstacles begins with self-awareness—recognizing the biases that shape your interactions and taking conscious steps to set them aside.

In demanding environments, emotional fatigue and burnout can hinder empathy. Here, self-care and boundary-setting become essential. Ensuring you have the emotional resources to engage empathetically without depleting yourself allows for more meaningful connections with others.

Everyday Empathy

The Dalai Lama's teachings and actions reflect his deep commitment to empathy. He often speaks about the importance of understanding others' suffering and perspectives, stressing that this is the foundation of compassion. His ability to listen actively is evident in his interactions with people from various walks of life, from world leaders to ordinary citizens, where he engages with genuine curiosity and concern.

His empathetic leadership style has allowed him to advocate effectively for the rights of the Tibetan people and promote global peace. His message resonates in numerous international forums, where he speaks about the importance of emotional and spiritual well-being, fostering an environment of mutual respect and understanding across diverse global communities.

Everyday interactions offer countless opportunities to practice empathy, turning routine exchanges into moments of genuine connection. For instance, engaging in empathetic conversations with colleagues can transform the workplace into a supportive and collaborative environment. Similarly, demonstrating empathy in customer service interactions enhances the customer experience, fostering loyalty and trust. These moments, though seemingly small, have the power to ripple outward, creating a culture of empathy that extends far beyond the individual interaction.

By embracing empathy daily, you contribute to a world where understanding and compassion are the norm, not the exception.

Empathy in Conflict Resolution

In conflict situations, especially those involving deep emotions or differing viewpoints, empathy can help transform adversarial interactions into more co-operative and solution-oriented discussions. When individuals in conflict empathize with each other, they are more likely to listen actively, acknowledge the emotional stakes, and be open to compromise rather than becoming defensive or entrenched in their positions. One key aspect of empathy in conflict resolution is that it shifts the focus from a "win-lose" mentality to a more collaborative "win-win" approach. Rather than seeing the other person as an opponent, empathizing allows one to perceive them as a human being with valid experiences and feelings, which can defuse tension and pave the way for constructive dialogue.

An empathic approach involves not just hearing the words the other person is saying but also understanding their underlying emotions, fears, and needs. This is essential for addressing the root causes of the conflict rather than just the superficial symptoms. Empathy enables individuals to step outside of their own perspective and gain insights into the experiences and motivations of others. By doing so, they can identify common ground and find solutions that meet the interests of both parties rather than settling for a solution that benefits only one side. In addition, empathy can lead to more positive and lasting resolutions because it fosters mutual respect and builds trust between the parties involved.

A real-life example of empathy in conflict resolution can be seen in the process of restorative justice, particularly in the context of criminal justice. Restorative justice focuses on repairing the harm caused by criminal behavior through dialogue between the victim and the offender, often with the help of a mediator. In many cases, the victim feels anger, betrayal, or fear, while the offender may struggle with guilt or defensiveness. Through the process, both parties are encouraged to share their feelings and perspectives in a safe, structured environment. The mediator facilitates this exchange by encouraging active listening and empathy, helping each side understand the other's emotional experience. For instance, in a therapeutic justice session involving a victim of theft and the offender, the victim might express feelings of violation and loss. In contrast, the offender might explain their struggles, such as poverty or addiction, which led to the crime. By recognizing the humanity in both parties, empathy allows them to move beyond the anger or resentment that typically fuels conflict and open up to mutual understanding and healing. This empathetic exchange can result in agreements about how to make amends, whether through apologies, restitution, or community service and can reduce the likelihood of reoffending. The success of restorative justice illustrates how, when applied thoughtfully in conflict resolution, empathy can foster healing, accountability, and stronger relationships in the aftermath of a dispute.

The Science of Active Listening

Imagine sitting across from a friend, nodding as they share a story about their day. You're present, but your mind drifts, caught in the web of your own thoughts. This is where active listening comes in—a skill that transforms passive hearing into meaningful engagement. At its core, active listening is about fully immersing yourself in the conversation, focusing entirely on the speaker rather than planning your response.

Active listening is an essential expression of empathy, enabling you to understand better and connect with others. It involves several key components:

- **Minimizing distractions**—putting away your phone, turning off the TV, and making eye contact signaling your commitment to the conversation.
- **Verbal affirmations**, such as simple nods or exclamations like "I see" or "Go on," encourage the speaker and show that you are engaged.

- **Non-verbal cues** such as leaning forward, maintaining an open posture, and mirroring the speaker's expressions reinforce the connection.

Mastering active listening requires intentional practice. One effective method is mindfulness—taking a moment before entering a conversation to center yourself. Focus on your breath to clear your mind of distractions. This mindfulness practice grounds you in the moment, enhancing your ability to listen with intent.

Additionally, techniques for avoiding interruptive thoughts are key. When your mind begins to wander, gently redirect your focus back to the speaker, using their words as an anchor. Recognizing these moments without judgment allows you to return to the conversation with renewed attention.

Tone & Inflection in Active Listening

Tone and inflection are critical elements in active listening because they influence how messages are received, interpreted, and responded to. These vocal cues can either enhance or hinder the communication process, shaping the emotional quality of the interaction and contributing to its success or failure.

Tone refers to the overall quality or character of one's voice, which can convey a range of emotions such as warmth, aggression, sarcasm, enthusiasm, or indifference. In active listening, the listener's tone can signal to the speaker whether they are engaged, open and empathetic. For example, a soft, calm and steady tone indicates attentiveness and reassurance, while a harsh or dismissive tone might suggest judgment or impatience. When listening actively, a listener's tone of voice can help reassure the speaker that they are in a safe and non-judgmental space, which is essential for fostering trust and open dialogue.

Conversely, inflection refers to the rise and fall in pitch while speaking, and it can dramatically affect how a message is perceived. A listener's inflection can signal interest, surprise, confusion, or agreement, depending on how the voice rises or falls in response to the speaker. For instance, if a listener's voice increases slightly at the end of a sentence, it can indicate curiosity or a desire for clarification, whereas a downward inflection can signal understanding or affirmation. When a listener adjusts their inflection to reflect the emotional undertones of the speaker's message, it helps to validate the speaker's feelings and encourages them to continue sharing. This kind of vocal responsiveness demonstrates that the listener is not only hearing the words but also attuned to the speaker's emotional state and the nuances of their message.

Together, tone and inflection help convey non-verbal feedback, which we know is often more powerful than the words themselves. When these vocal cues align with the content of the conversation, they create a sense of connection and mutual respect. For example, if a speaker is discussing a sensitive or painful topic, a listener who responds with a gentle, warm tone and uses soft, understanding inflections can make the speaker feel supported and validated. On the other hand, a tone that is abrupt, dismissive, or monotone can cause the speaker to feel disregarded or frustrated, even if the listener's words are neutral or polite.

Feedback and Clarification

Feedback is a vital component of active listening. Paraphrasing and summarizing what you've heard confirms your comprehension while allowing the speaker to clarify or expand on their points. For example, you might say, "So what I'm hearing is..." or "It sounds like you're saying..." This shows your engagement and ensures that the message has been accurately received.

Asking clarifying questions further deepens the conversation. Questions like "Can you tell me more about that?" or "How did that make you feel?" show a genuine interest in their perspective, inviting them to elaborate.

Responding with Emotional Intelligence

In a world where emotions often drive our interactions, emotional intelligence (EI) is a linchpin for effective communication. EI refers to the ability to recognize, understand, and manage your own emotions while also comprehending the feelings of others. This dual capability forms the foundation for meaningful, empathetic responses in conversations.

Recognizing your emotions provides insight into the triggers that evoke certain feelings and reactions. This awareness helps regulate your responses, preventing impulsive actions that might escalate a situation. Understanding the emotions of others further enhances this process by allowing you to tailor your responses to their emotional state, fostering a deeper connection.

When responding, validating the other person's feelings is an essential emotional intelligence skill. For example, saying, "I can see you're upset about this," acknowledges their emotions without judgment. In difficult conversations, compassion is key. Compassionate responses, characterized by empathy and support, can de-escalate tension and encourage collaboration. Instead of jumping into problem-solving, you might say, "How can I support you right now?" This shifts the focus from fixing the problem to offering emotional support.

Building Trust Through Empathetic Engagement

In relationships, trust is built on empathetic interactions. When you consistently demonstrate empathy, you show others that you value their feelings and perspectives. This fosters a sense of safety and openness, encouraging honesty and vulnerability. For example, in one of the teams I worked with, we had a member named Helen who had been unusually quiet in meetings. Her ideas were often overlooked, and while she seemed to withdraw, she had relevant insights to contribute. One day, during a particularly tense brainstorming session, I noticed her reluctance to speak up. Rather than pressuring her to share, I approached her privately after the meeting, acknowledging that she seemed hesitant to contribute and asking if something was on her mind.

She opened up about feeling dismissed in earlier discussions, where her ideas hadn't been given proper consideration, making her less confident in speaking up. Rather than defending the team's behavior, I listened, validating her feelings. I said, "I can understand why you'd feel that way. It must be frustrating to feel your input isn't valued." By giving her the space to express her frustrations and showing empathy, I helped her feel heard. At the next meeting, Helen felt empowered to share her thoughts, and her contributions turned out to be a pivotal turning point for the project. From then on, Helen was much more engaged in discussions, and her trust in the team grew, leading to stronger collaboration.

Empathy is not just about listening—sometimes, it's about creating the right environment for someone to feel comfortable opening up. This simple act of recognition, validation, and encouragement can transform someone's relationship with the group.

Building trust through empathetic communication requires consistency. Keeping promises, no matter how small, reinforces reliability and integrity. When you follow through on commitments, you show others they can count on you, deepening their trust.

However, trust can be fragile, and breaches—whether intentional or accidental—can damage relationships. To repair trust, acknowledge mistakes, take responsibility, and make amends. Balancing openness with appropriate boundaries is also important, ensuring that trust evolves without overexposure or discomfort.

Building trust through empathetic engagement is an ongoing process. By practicing empathy in every interaction, you strengthen your connections with others, creating relationships that are resilient, open, and built on mutual understanding. In the next chapter, we will explore the balance between speaking and listening, further enhancing your communication skills and deepening your relationships.

Checklist for Empathy & Active Listening

Use this checklist as a guide to assess your empathetic engagement in conversations.

- I created a safe space for the other person to express themselves.
- I actively listened without interrupting or planning my response while they spoke.
- I acknowledged the other person's feelings or experiences without judgment.
- I avoided jumping to conclusions or offering advice too quickly.
- I shared my feelings or vulnerabilities to create a reciprocal, trusting environment.
- I asked open-ended questions to encourage deeper dialogue and understanding.
- I used reflective listening (e.g., paraphrasing or summarizing their words) to confirm understanding.
- I validated the other person's perspective, even if I didn't fully agree.
- I showed patience and gave the other person the time they needed to articulate their thoughts.
- I followed up with actions or promises to show that I value their trust.

7

BALANCING SPEAKING AND LISTENING

"Listening is not a skill, it's a discipline. All you have to do is keep your mouth shut." Peter Drucker

You will notice that I touch on the topic of 'attentive listening' in both chapters 6 and 7. This is deliberate, because 'attentive listening' plays a very important role in all conversations. It is a key lesson that cannot be emphasized enough. I have put a different slant on each example to enhance the message. I hope you will agree that repetition is beneficial when learning something new.

Picture yourself at a dinner party, engaged in a lively discussion about a recent film. As the conversation flows, you notice one person dominating the dialogue, leaving little room for others to contribute. You want to interject, to share your thoughts, but you're unsure when or how. This common scenario highlights the delicate relationship between speaking and listening that defines effective communication. Achieving this balance is crucial. It ensures all voices are heard, ideas are exchanged, and connections are formed.

Conversations are not just about speaking or listening but about knowing when to do each.

When we fail to maintain this equilibrium, misunderstandings arise.

Imagine a team meeting where one member speaks over others, pushing their agenda without pause. Important ideas are lost, and frustration builds. This imbalance not only stifles creativity but also strains relationships. On the other hand, a conversation where everyone is given space to contribute fosters a sense of inclusion and respect. Equal communication creates an environment where people feel valued and understood, laying the groundwork for stronger connections. It transforms dialogue into a collaborative exchange, where each participant's insights enrich the discussion.

Deciding when to speak involves assessing the relevance and value of your contribution. Ask yourself, "Does this add to the conversation?" or "Is this the right time to share?" Consider whether your input will enhance the dialogue or shift it off course.

Timing is crucial. Speaking up at the right moment can emphasize a point, while poorly timed interjections may disrupt the flow.

Context also matters. In professional settings, concise and relevant contributions are often more impactful. In casual conversations, sharing personal stories might foster deeper connections. Balancing these elements ensures your voice is heard without overshadowing others.

Recognizing when to listen is equally important. Pay attention to verbal cues that suggest openness or the need for further exploration, such as pauses or questions. As mentioned previously, non-verbal signals, like nodding or leaning forward, indicate engagement, suggesting the speaker values your input. Observing the dynamics of the conversation helps gauge when listening is more beneficial. If someone is sharing a personal experience or complex idea, your role may be to absorb and understand rather than respond immediately.

This attentiveness deepens your understanding and strengthens the relationship, demonstrating respect.

Practicing Balance in Conversation

Engage in a role-playing exercise with a partner, alternating between speaker and listener. Choose a topic of mutual interest. As one person speaks, the other practices active listening, offering feedback and asking questions. Afterward, switch roles and reflect on the experience. Discuss what techniques helped maintain balance and what could be improved. This practice enhances your awareness of conversational dynamics, helping you find the right mix of speaking and listening in future interactions.

Participating in group discussions with a focus on balance also hones these skills. Encourage each member to share their thoughts, promoting an environment where all voices are valued. This collaborative approach enriches the discussion and builds a culture of mutual respect. As you practice, notice how the balance of speaking and listening influences the quality of the conversation. Embrace the pauses, the exchanges and the insights that emerge when dialogue flows naturally.

Techniques for Encouraging Others to Share

Imagine yourself in a room where everyone's thoughts hang in the air, waiting to be spoken. It's a space where encouragement isn't just a nicety but a tool for connection. Inviting others to share their thoughts nurtures inclusivity, creating an environment where everyone feels valued. This encouragement fosters a supportive atmosphere where ideas flourish and relationships deepen. When people feel encouraged to speak, discussions become richer, more dynamic, and filled with diverse perspectives. It's like adding different colors to a painting, each hue contributing to a more vibrant picture. Encouragement allows us to hear voices that might otherwise remain silent.

To prompt others to share, start with open-ended questions that invite elaboration. Instead of asking yes-or-no questions, consider, "What are your thoughts on this?" or "How do you feel about that?" These questions open the door for others to express themselves freely without the constraints of a limited answer. They show genuine interest in the other person's perspective, encouraging them to contribute more deeply to the conversation. Non-verbal cues also play a crucial role. Simple actions like nodding or maintaining eye contact signal that you're engaged and receptive. These gestures create a sense of safety, reassuring the speaker that their words are welcome and valued.

Creating a safe space for sharing is vital for encouraging openness. This involves demonstrating empathy and understanding through active listening as discussed in the previous chapter. When someone speaks, listen not just to reply but to understand. Acknowledge their feelings and thoughts without judgment, creating an environment where they feel comfortable sharing more. Avoiding interruptions is important. Allow pauses in the conversation to unfold naturally, giving the speaker time to gather their thoughts. Patience in these moments shows respect and encourages others to express themselves without fearing being cut off.

I recently coached a teacher who couldn't get classroom interaction off the ground. He was unaware that he always asked the same students for a response. As a result, others remained silent, believing he wasn't interested in their input. His classroom discussions transformed when he invited every student to share their diverse opinions and ideas. These conversations led to a series of stories that brought the class closer together, revealing insights that might have otherwise remained hidden. This illustrates how encouragement can empower individuals to speak up, turning conversations into vibrant exchanges.

Managing Dominance in Conversations

I'm sure we've all been in a meeting where one person talks incessantly, leaving no room for others to contribute. This is conversational dominance, where a single voice overshadows the rest, often stifling dialogue and creativity. It can turn a collaborative environment into a one-sided monologue, where diverse ideas and perspectives are lost.

Dominance can be subtle, such as interrupting frequently or steering every topic back to oneself. It can also manifest overtly, like dismissing others' opinions or speaking over them. These behaviors disrupt the balance necessary for effective communication, leading to participant frustration and disengagement. The effects on group dynamics are profound. When one person dominates, others may retreat, feeling their contributions aren't valued. This imbalance hinders the flow of ideas and impacts morale as people become reluctant to share. Over time, this can erode trust and cooperation within a group, stalling progress and innovation.

To manage dominance, self-awareness is key. It's important to recognize when your voice is overpowering the conversation. This requires honest reflection on your communication habits. Are you speaking more than listening?
Do you often interrupt or redirect discussions back to yourself?
By acknowledging these patterns, you can begin to adjust your approach.

One technique is to set personal limits on your speaking time, allowing space for others to share. This might involve consciously pausing after making a point and inviting others to contribute. It could also mean actively listening more, focusing on understanding rather than responding immediately. Creating a mental checklist can help keep these goals in mind, fostering a more inclusive dialogue.

Facilitation plays a crucial role in mitigating dominance. A skilled facilitator can guide discussions, ensuring all voices are heard. This involves redirecting focus to quieter participants and encouraging them to share their insights.
Phrases like "I'd love to hear your thoughts on this" or "What do you think about this perspective?" can be powerful invitations for those who hesitate to speak up. Encouraging equitable contribution from all members diversifies the conversation and enriches the dialogue with various perspectives and ideas.

Practicing non-dominance can be developed through specific exercises. Group activities where roles rotate between speaker and listener can provide valuable practice. Each participant takes turns speaking and listening in these scenarios, offering feedback on the experience. This highlights the importance of balance and enhances understanding of the dynamics at play.

Observing and reflecting on personal communication habits is another effective strategy. Keep a journal of your interactions, noting moments where you felt dominant or where others were. Reflect on what triggered these behaviors and how you might adjust.

By addressing conversational dominance, we pave the way for richer, more inclusive interactions. It requires a commitment to self-awareness, a willingness to adapt, and a focus on fostering a collaborative environment. The benefits are manifold, from improved group dynamics to enhanced creativity and innovation. As we learn to manage dominance, we create spaces where every voice is valued, every idea is heard, and every conversation becomes an opportunity for connection and growth.

Handling Conflict in Communication

Conflict is an inevitable part of life, whether in personal relationships, the workplace, or everyday interactions. While conflict itself isn't inherently negative, how we handle it can determine the outcome. If approached thoughtfully and with a focus on resolution, conflict can lead to greater understanding, stronger relationships, and creative solutions. However, when emotions are high, conflict can quickly escalate if we don't take care to balance speaking and listening. In these situations, managing our emotional responses and maintaining composure is crucial for keeping the conversation productive and resolving the issue effectively.

When emotions run high, the instinct is often to defend ourselves or react to perceived attacks. However, reacting impulsively can escalate the conflict, making it more difficult to reach a resolution. Instead, focusing on listening first—without interruption—helps defuse tension and allows for a more rational conversation.

For instance, imagine a workplace disagreement between two colleagues, Anna and Mike, over a project. Anna feels that Mike has not been pulling his weight, while Mike believes that Anna is micromanaging and undermining his ideas. If both start defending their positions immediately, the conversation will become combative and unproductive. However, if Anna listens attentively to Mike's concerns without interrupting, she might understand the deeper reasons for his frustration. This allows both to move toward a solution without needing to "win" the argument.

Active listening in conflict resolution means paying full attention, acknowledging the other person's feelings, and reflecting back their concerns to show that you understand. It can be as simple as saying, "I hear you're frustrated because you feel like your contributions aren't being valued." This step can calm the emotional temperature of the conversation and open space for dialogue.

De-escalating Tension in Heated Conversations

Learning to de-escalate tension is an invaluable skill. When emotions are high, responding with anger or defensiveness only fuels the fire. Instead, pausing before responding can help maintain control of the conversation. Taking a moment to breathe deeply and collect your thoughts helps avoid impulsive reactions that might escalate the situation.

For example, in a heated discussion about household chores between two roommates, one person might raise their voice and express frustration about not being helped enough. The other might feel attacked and instantly respond with anger. However, if the second roommate pauses, takes a breath, and chooses to react calmly, both individuals can reconsider their approach. Saying something like," I understand you're upset about the chores, and I want to find a way to work this out together," can create a shift in tone and open space for compromise.

Conflict resolution is not about winning or being right; it's about understanding the issue, acknowledging emotions, and working together to find a solution. By focusing on listening, de-escalating tension, and staying composed, we can resolve conflicts to strengthen relationships and promote understanding.

Cultivating a Dialogic Mindset

Think of conversations like a dance, where both partners move in harmony, responding to each other's cues. This is the essence of a dialogic mindset—viewing conversations as cooperative exchanges rather than combative encounters.

In this approach, the goal is not to win or dominate but to understand and connect. We open the door to richer and more meaningful interactions when we foster a cooperative communication environment. Dialogic conversations thrive on mutual engagement, where each person is both a speaker and a listener, contributing to a shared understanding. This stands in stark contrast to adversarial interactions, where the focus is on outtalking or outsmarting the other person. In such cases, the conversation becomes a battleground, with each party trying to assert their point rather than seeking common ground.

Shifting to a dialogic mindset requires consciously prioritizing mutual understanding over individual agendas. One way to develop this approach is by practicing curiosity and open-mindedness in discussions. Enter conversations with the intention to learn, asking questions that invite exploration rather than confrontation. This might involve setting aside preconceived notions and allowing yourself to be surprised by the other person's perspective.

Prioritizing shared goals also plays a crucial role. When you focus on what you and the other person are trying to achieve together, aligning your efforts and working collaboratively becomes easier. This shift from a "me" mindset to a "we" mindset transforms the dynamic, fostering cooperation and connection.

Flexibility and adaptability are key components of a dialogic mindset. Being open to changing perspectives enhances dialogue by allowing space for new ideas to emerge. It's about remaining receptive to what you hear, even if it challenges your beliefs. Techniques for staying open include active listening, focusing intently on the speaker without planning your response, and reflective thinking, considering how new information might alter your views. Numerous examples illustrate flexibility leading to innovative solutions. In a team meeting, for instance, a manager might initially resist a new strategy but, through open dialogue, realize its potential and decides to implement it. Such adaptability enriches the conversation and fosters a culture of innovation and growth.

Reflecting on your communication style is an important step in cultivating a dialogic mindset. Start by journaling reflections on past interactions, focusing on the quality of dialogue. Consider questions like:
Did I approach this conversation with an open mind?
Was I more interested in understanding or being understood?
This self-reflection can reveal patterns and areas for improvement.

Seeking feedback from peers is also valuable. Invite trusted colleagues, friends or your coach to share their observations of your communication style and be open to their insights. This external perspective can highlight blind spots and offer guidance on how to enhance your dialogic skills.

A dialogic mindset transforms conversations into opportunities for connection and growth. By approaching dialogue as a collaborative exchange, you create a space where every voice is valued and every perspective is considered. This mindset enriches your interactions and deepens your relationships, fostering a sense of unity and understanding. As you embrace this approach, you'll find that your conversations become more fulfilling and impactful, setting the stage for richer connections and more significant insights.

With this foundation, you're ready to explore the next chapter, where we delve into the complexities of networking and career advancement.

Self-Assessment : Balance of Speaking & Listening

Instructions: For each question, rate yourself on a scale from 1 to 5

1 = Rarely 2 = Occasionally 3 = Sometimes 4 = Often 5 = Always

Do I allow others to finish their thoughts completely before responding?

Do I find it difficult to listen without mentally preparing my response?

Do I reflect on or paraphrase what the speaker has said to confirm my understanding?

Do I prioritize the quality of listening over the need to express my opinions in discussions?

Do I actively listen for both verbal and nonverbal cues to understand the whole message being communicated?

How often do I find myself dominating conversations by speaking more than listening?

How frequently do I ask follow-up questions to clarify or deepen my understanding of what others are saying?

When someone is speaking, how often do I notice myself becoming distracted or thinking about unrelated topics?

How often do I interrupt others during conversations to share my own thoughts or opinions?

When I disagree with someone, how likely am I to listen fully before explaining my perspective?

How often do I offer verbal affirmations (like "I understand" or "Tell me more") to show I am engaged in a conversation?

When a conversation ends, how often do I feel that both parties had an equal opportunity to speak and be heard?

Scoring and Reflection
Add up your scores for a total out of 60.

48–60: You likely have a strong balance between speaking and listening.

36–47: You may strike a balance occasionally but could improve active listening or speaking behaviors.

12–35: You might benefit from focusing more on either listening or limiting interruptions.

8

NETWORKING AND CAREER ADVANCEMENT

"What makes networking work is that it sets up win-win situations in which all parties involved get to take something home." Earl G Graves Snr

You are standing in a crowded elevator surrounded by colleagues and strangers. The space is tight, everyone is silent, and you have only the duration of that elevator ride to make an impression. This is where the elevator pitch concept originates—a brief, impactful introduction designed to spark interest and initiate further conversation. Crafting an elevator pitch that resonates is an art, and it starts with understanding the core components:

a crisp introduction
a compelling value proposition
a clear call to action

These elements must fit seamlessly into a 30-second narrative, capturing attention without overwhelming the listener.

Your introduction is the first handshake, even if it's just verbal. It sets the tone, offers a glimpse into who you are, and establishes the initial connection. Think of it as the opening line of a novel—it should intrigue and invite curiosity. The value proposition is where you shine, illustrating what you bring to the table. It's about articulating your unique strengths and skills, which differentiate you in your field or industry. This isn't just about listing achievements but weaving them into a story that speaks directly to the needs or interests of your audience. Finally, the call to action is your invitation, whether it's a request for a meeting, a suggestion for collaboration, or a simple invite to continue the conversation. It guides the listener on what to do next, ensuring the dialogue doesn't end with the ding of the elevator doors.

Identifying your unique value proposition requires introspection and honesty. Start by pinpointing your core skills and strengths. What do you excel at? What comes naturally to you? Reflect on past experiences where you've made a significant impact. These moments often hold the key to your unique value. Consider how these strengths align with the needs of your audience. Tailoring your pitch involves adapting language and examples to suit the context, ensuring relevance and clarity. Avoid industry jargon that might alienate or confuse. Instead, focus on clear, relatable language that resonates with your listener's experiences and challenges. Consider how your skills can solve a problem or enhance an opportunity specific to them.

Practicing and refining your elevator pitch is essential for polish and confidence. One effective technique is to record your pitch and review it. Listening to your delivery can reveal areas for improvement, whether in tone, pace, or emphasis. Role-playing scenarios with peers or mentors offer another layer of feedback. Choose different contexts, such as a networking event or a casual meet-up and adjust your pitch accordingly. This exercise helps refine your message and builds adaptability for real-world applications. By rehearsing in varied situations, you hone your ability to pivot and personalize your pitch on the spot, making it both engaging and effective.

The elevator pitch is more than a professional necessity; it's a personal declaration of who you are and what you aspire to achieve. It distills your essence into a concise narrative, inviting others to join you on your journey. In crafting and delivering your pitch, you gain clarity about your goals and the value you offer, empowering you to navigate networking and career advancement confidently and purposefully.

Exercise: Perfecting Your Elevator Pitch

Grab a notebook and jot down the main elements of your pitch: an engaging introduction, your unique value proposition, and a clear call to action. Record yourself delivering this pitch. Listen critically, focusing on clarity, tone and timing. Adjust where necessary and then rehearse with a trusted friend or mentor. Ask for honest feedback, and refine your pitch based on their insights. Repeat this process until your elevator pitch feels natural and compelling. I've created an Elevator Pitch Template for you to follow at the end of this chapter.

Building a Professional Network Strategically

Networking is often likened to an intricate and interconnected web where each thread strengthens the overall structure. Strategic networking, however, is about creating that web with intention. Instead of casting a wide net haphazardly, it involves pinpointing opportunities that align with your goals and values. For example, attending an industry seminar where every conversation holds potential. Here, networking isn't just about collecting business cards; it's about forging relationships that matter.

In today's fast-paced world, where career advancement hinges on who you know as much as what you know, understanding the role of networking is pivotal. A robust network opens doors to opportunities, offering support, guidance, and access to resources that can propel your career forward. It's the difference between passively hoping for connections and actively cultivating them.

You must identify these opportunities to build a network that genuinely supports your ambitions. Industry conferences and seminars are fertile grounds for meeting like-minded professionals. These events are designed to unite individuals with shared interests, creating a space ripe for connection. Engage actively in discussions, attend workshops and participate in panels. Each interaction is a chance to learn, share and find those who resonate with your professional journey.

Online platforms, too, offer vast potential. Professional communities and forums allow you to engage with peers globally, breaking geographical boundaries. Through these digital spaces, you can join conversations, contribute insights and expand your network beyond physical confines.

Making meaningful connections requires more than just showing up; it demands genuine curiosity. Approach new contacts with an open mind, eager to understand their experiences and perspectives. Ask questions that encourage dialogue, not just responses. Finding common ground through shared challenges or aspirations creates a foundation of mutual respect and interest. As you engage, look for ways to contribute value. Identifying how you can support others fosters a sense of community and collaboration. It's about building relationships where both parties feel enriched, paving the way for long-term connections.

The role of giving in networking cannot be overstated. Offering value to your contacts through sharing resources, insights, or introductions strengthens your network, encourages reciprocity and enriches everyone's experience. If someone mentions a challenge they're facing and you have relevant expertise, offer your insights or suggest resources that might help.

Introducing new contacts to beneficial connections is always appreciated and can open doors for them and enhance your network's diversity. It's a reciprocal exchange where each party contributes to and benefits from the collective knowledge and opportunities. By focusing on what you can give rather than what you can gain, you build a network founded on trust and collaboration that will last.

Navigating Networking Events with Ease

Walking into a networking event can feel like stepping into a whirlwind. Preparation is your ally in navigating this type of environment.

Before attending, take a moment to set clear objectives for what you hope to achieve. Are you there to meet potential collaborators, explore career opportunities, or gain insights into industry trends? Knowing your goals helps direct your focus and energy. Crafting a practical introduction and conversation starters tailored to the event can also ease initial interactions. Think of a few key points you'd like to convey about yourself or your work and be ready with questions that invite others to share their experiences.

Once inside, engaging with confidence becomes the name of the game. Approach groups and individuals openly, signaling your willingness to connect. A warm smile and genuine interest in others go a long way in breaking the ice. When initiating conversations, remember that active listening is your greatest tool. It keeps you grounded and fosters a deeper connection with those around you. Listen intently to what others say and respond thoughtfully, weaving shared interests or goals into the dialogue. This approach builds rapport and makes interactions more memorable for both parties. As you engage, be mindful of the natural flow of conversation, allowing it to evolve organically rather than forcing it in a particular direction. This flexibility eases the pressure on you and creates a relaxed atmosphere for everyone involved.

While rich with opportunity, networking events come with their challenges. Anxiety or nervousness is common, especially in large gatherings where the sheer number of people can be overwhelming. Take a moment to breathe and remind yourself of your objectives. Visualize successful interactions, focusing on the positive outcomes you hope to achieve.

Navigating cliques or exclusive groups can be confronting. These tight-knit circles may seem impenetrable, but approaching them with humility, respect and a smile can open doors. Introducing yourself and expressing interest in their conversation can gradually break down barriers. It's about finding the right moment and showing genuine interest in what they say.

I remember being introduced to an event organizer at a coaching conference a few years ago. We chatted briefly, but he had to leave in a hurry. At first, I thought he wasn't interested in talking to me. I was hesitant to ask for his business card, but I did before he darted off. Even though I felt nervous, I contacted him the next day and we arranged a coffee meeting. We kept in touch online and a few months later, he offered me the opportunity to speak at his firm. I was surprised and delighted. This transformation from a casual encounter to a career opportunity underpins the importance of being present, staying in touch and remaining open to possibilities.

When my daughter finished university, I encouraged her to attend a local networking event for young entrepreneurs because I know the power of such gatherings. She was nervous and unsure of what to expect but went armed with a few questions and genuine enthusiasm. Her proactive engagement caught the attention of a leading industry expert who after chatting with her, recognized her potential and offered her a coveted internship.

These true stories highlight how networking can be a catalyst for growth, turning fleeting exchanges into lasting relationships and wonderful opportunities.

The Art of Follow-Up: Sustaining Connections

You've just left a networking event with a stack of business cards in your pocket. Each one represents a potential relationship, a door left ajar. But without follow-up, these opportunities can fade into oblivion. Timely follow-up is crucial; it solidifies the initial impression and demonstrates sincere interest. It prevents those connections from slipping through the cracks, ensuring the dialogue continues beyond that fleeting first encounter. Without it, even the most promising introductions can wither, leaving untapped potential.

Crafting effective follow-up communication is an art and must not be ignored. A personalized follow-up email or message is more than a courtesy; it's a reaffirmation of interest and a gentle nudge toward further engagement. Begin by referencing your previous conversation, showing you were genuinely interested in what was shared. This helps jog their memory and re-establishes the context of your meeting. Then, suggest specific reasons for future collaboration or meetings. Perhaps you discussed a shared interest, a project that aligns with your goals, or an event that could benefit you both. Highlighting these points provides a reason to reconnect and underscores the value of your budding relationship.

Balancing persistence with patience is critical in follow-up communications. While staying on their radar is important, you must avoid appearing overly eager or intrusive, which can be off-putting. Timing is everything. Gauge the appropriate follow-up interval based on industry norms and the nature of your initial interaction. In some fields, a week might be customary, while a more immediate follow-up could be expected in others. If you're anxious, do it immediately before you change your mind. That's what I do.

Recognize when it's time to pause or shift focus to other opportunities. If a contact doesn't respond after a couple of attempts, it might be wise to step back and revisit the connection later. This demonstrates respect for their time and space, preserving the relationship for future re-engagement.

Long-term relationship building requires a system for nurturing and maintaining your network over time. Regularly checking in with contacts through updates or shared content keeps you relevant in their minds without the need for constant direct communication. Whether it's sharing an article that might interest them, congratulating them on a recent achievement, or simply sending a friendly message during the holidays, these touch points strengthen the foundation of your relationship. Celebrating achievements and milestones together fosters a sense of camaraderie and mutual respect. Acknowledging their successes shows that you value them beyond the professional sphere, enriching the connection and laying the groundwork for deeper collaboration.

I know networking events can be stressful, especially for those of you who feel overwhelmed by large groups or find it challenging to converse with strangers. I understand that the pressure to make a good impression, navigate small talk, or advocate for yourself can feel daunting. However, these events are crucial for personal and professional growth. It's okay to acknowledge your anxiety—it's a natural response to stepping outside your comfort zone. But rather than avoiding the discomfort, I encourage you to lean into it. Remember that every interaction is a chance to learn; the more you show up, the easier it will become. Courage grows with action, so take a deep breath, go, and trust your ability to navigate the experience.

Here's the elevator pitch outline – remember you only have 30 seconds to connect with everyone and let them know who you are, what you do and why they should take your business card or meet you for coffee next week. Learn it off by heart so you don't sound nervous or forget what to say.

Elevator Pitch Template

Introduction: Start with your name and your role.

Example: "Good evening, my name is Anne McKeown, I'm a Communication Coach who empowers people to step up, speak up and show up with confidence in business and life."

Engagement: Open with a question or statement that highlights common challenges.

Example: "Have you ever felt overlooked in conversations or struggled to articulate your thoughts in high-pressure situations?"

The Need: Describe the common issues people face that your business addresses.

Example: "Many talented professionals find themselves unable to speak up in meetings, manage small talk, or connect deeply with colleagues and clients."

Your Approach: Explain your unique answer or philosophy.

Example:"Using a blend of personalized strategies and practical exercises, I help clients find their authentic voice and communicate with clarity in all situations."

Success Stories: Briefly mention a success story or a general outcome experienced by your clients.

Example: "Clients who have worked with me have gone on to lead teams more effectively, engage more confidently in networking events, and even excel in public speaking."

The Benefit: State the direct benefits your role/company provides to potential clients.

Example: "With my coaching, you can expect to feel heard and understood, build stronger relationships at work and home, and finally feel at ease in conversations, no matter the setting."

The Ask: Conclude with what you seek, such as new clients, a workshop opportunity, or a speaking engagement.

Example: "I'm looking to expand my client base with professionals eager to transform their communicative abilities."

Closing: Thank the listener for their time and suggest a way to continue the conversation.

Example: "Thank you for your time. I'd love to exchange contact information and learn more about your business."

And remember to smile.

9

ENHANCING MEMORY AND RECALL

"A person's name to them is the sweetest sound." Dale Carnegie

You're at a lively gathering and as you circulate the room, you meet several new people. Each introduction feels like an opportunity, yet you struggle to remember their names moments after they've spoken. It's a common scenario that can unsettle even the most confident of us.

The ability to remember names isn't just a party trick; it's a crucial skill that can forge stronger personal connections and leave lasting impressions. Recalling a name is a simple yet profound gesture that shows respect and attentiveness. We all love it when the local barista remembers our name and coffee order; this recognition makes us feel a sense of belonging.

In professional settings, this ability becomes even more essential. Remembering colleagues' and clients' names can set the tone for future interactions and foster trust and connection.

Mnemonic Techniques for Name Recall

So, how can we remember the names of multiple people? My secret weapon is alliteration. I pair a person's name with an easily memorable characteristic or profession. For instance, "Tom the Teacher" or "Lisa from

London" creates a catchy phrase that links the name to something tangible and makes it much easier for me to remember.

Associating names with visual imagery is another excellent technique. If I were to meet someone named Rose, I'd picture a rose flower alongside her face. A vivid image like this anchors her name in my memory, making retrieving it later easier. These devices act as mental shortcuts, transforming abstract names into memorable concepts your brain can easily access.

Another thing I do is repeat the person's name several times during the initial conversation to embed it in my brain. I greet them using their name, include their name when asking them questions, and I even mention it as we part ways to reinforce it in my memory. Writing down names immediately after introductions can also strengthen recall, whether in a discreet notebook or a notes app on your phone. The more you practice these strategies, the more natural they will become.

Attentiveness plays a big role in remembering names. When someone introduces themselves, focus on their name as if it's the most vital part of the conversation. This requires minimizing distractions and giving them your full attention. Listen with intent and maintain eye contact. Reduce distractions by putting your phone away, avoid letting your gaze wander, and center your attention on the person and create a mental space where their name can take root. This practice of mindfulness not only aids memory but also demonstrates genuine interest, setting a positive tone for the interaction.

Creating Mental Hooks: Associative Memory Techniques

Associative memory is a fascinating aspect of our cognitive function, intertwining different pieces of information to make them easier to recall. Imagine your brain as a vast library, where each piece of information is a book on a shelf. Associative memory acts like a librarian who remembers where each book is and how they relate to each other. This ability to create mental links between concepts helps us store and retrieve information effectively. For instance, think about how a familiar song can instantly transport you back to a specific moment, evoking vivid memories and emotions. This is the power of association at work, creating a web of connections that your mind can easily navigate.

To develop personal mental hooks, consider linking new information with personal experiences. This approach transforms abstract concepts into relatable ones, making them more memorable. For example, if you're learning about a historical event, try associating it with a personal memory from a related location or period. This creates a unique anchor in your mind, allowing the new information to latch onto something familiar.

Rhymes and wordplay can also serve as effective mnemonic devices, turning complex information into catchy phrases that are easier to remember. Creating a rhyme or using alliteration can provide a rhythmic cue that jogs your memory when needed. These techniques tap into your brain's natural affinity for patterns and rhythm, making information stick.

Visualizing a "memory palace" is another technique that uses associative memory. This method involves mentally placing pieces of information within a familiar setting, like rooms in a house you know well. As you walk through the memory palace in your mind, each room or object you encounter triggers a specific piece of information, creating a vivid mental map.

Associating names with famous people or characters also works. Connecting a new name to someone well-known creates a mental shortcut that makes the name easier to recall. For example, if you meet someone named Albert, you might link them to Albert Einstein. This association provides a memorable reference point, helping the name resurface when needed.

I've created a Memory Palace Description and Quiz for you to try at the end of this chapter.

Implementation in Daily Life

Incorporating associative techniques into daily interactions can significantly enhance memory retention. Try creating associations for frequently encountered names or concepts, weaving them into stories or scenarios that resonate with you.

Practicing associations with lists or sets of new information can also be beneficial. When you encounter a list of items to remember, imagine them interacting in a creative scene. For example, you need to buy milk, potatoes, eggs, and bananas. Create a picture of bananas in pyjamas, Humpty Dumpty, and a couch potato crying over spilled milk. This transforms a mundane task into an engaging mental exercise that reinforces the connections you've made. Practicing these techniques regularly trains the brain to make associations naturally, turning memory retention into a fluid, intuitive process.

Memory, at its core, is about making connections. By harnessing the power of associative memory, you can transform how you store and recall information. These mental hooks make learning more engaging and enhance your ability to remember details that matter. Whether it's a name, a concept, or a set of instructions, associative memory techniques offer a dynamic way to deepen your understanding and retention.

Practicing Active Recall in Conversations

Have you ever been in a conversation where, halfway through, your mind draws a blank? And you struggle to remember the details you want to share, leaving you flustered? This is where active recall is terrific, offering a way to strengthen memory retention. Unlike passive review, which involves simply reading or hearing information multiple times, active recall pushes you to retrieve information actively from memory. This method engages your brain more deeply, reinforcing neural connections and making the information easier to recall later. Studies have shown that active recall significantly enhances memory retention compared to passive study methods[5]. It turns learning into an active process, requiring effort and engagement, which in turn cements the information in your mind more firmly.

Incorporating active recall into your conversations can transform how you remember details and engage with others. One effective technique is to summarize prior conversations before starting new ones. This practice reinforces your learning and prepares you for the next interaction. Imagine revisiting the main points of a previous discussion as you get ready to meet someone again. This habit keeps the information fresh and relevant, allowing you to build on it confidently. Quizzing yourself on key details after interactions is another powerful method. After a meeting or chat, take a moment to review the main topics discussed mentally. Challenge yourself to recall details like names, dates, or action items. This self-test reinforces your memory and helps identify gaps that need further attention.

Spaced Repetition

Revisiting information at intervals, rather than cramming it all at once, enhances long-term memory. This technique, known as spaced repetition, leverages the spacing effect—a phenomenon where information is better recalled when exposure is spaced out over time.

Creating a schedule for revisiting information is a practical way to incorporate this into your routine. Whether setting reminders on your phone or using a calendar, having a structured approach ensures you revisit key points regularly. Spaced repetition software or apps can also be beneficial, offering tailored schedules that adapt to your learning pace and retention needs. These tools guide you in revisiting information optimally, ensuring it remains accessible in your memory.

Engaging in memory games with friends or colleagues can be fun and practical to hone your active recall skills. These games challenge you to retrieve information in a dynamic setting, reinforcing your recall abilities.

Simple games like "20 Questions" or memory card matches can stimulate your mind and encourage quick recall.

Practicing recall through storytelling is another engaging exercise. Share a story or teach someone a concept, focusing on accurately recalling details. This method strengthens your memory and enhances your ability to communicate clearly and confidently. Teaching others requires a deep understanding of the material, pushing you to retrieve and organize information effectively.

As you explore these techniques, active recall will become a natural part of your conversational practice. Your effort in retrieving information pays off in more substantial, more reliable memories. Each conversation becomes an opportunity to reinforce what you've learned, turning memory retention into an engaging and rewarding process. By making active recall a habit, you unlock a powerful tool that enhances your interactions and enriches your understanding of the world.

Boosting Memory with Visualization Strategies

Visualization is a powerful tool that taps into the brain's ability to create and store vivid mental images, making it easier to remember information. Visualization engages the brain more fully by transforming abstract data into concrete images, enhancing retention and recall. The science behind this lies in how our mind processes images and relationships.

Visualization takes advantage of this natural inclination, converting words, numbers, or concepts into colorful, dynamic mental snapshots. When you visualize, you create a mental movie where each element plays a role, linking together to form a coherent, memorable scene. This technique can be a game-changer in learning and retaining complex information, turning dry facts into visual narratives.

Developing compelling visualizations requires some creativity and practice. Start by crafting detailed mental pictures for the information you want to remember. If you're trying to memorize a process, imagine each step as a scene in a movie. Use color to differentiate elements, movement to show progression, and emotion to highlight importance. For example, if you're learning about the water cycle, you might picture a vibrant blue river, the sun's warmth causing evaporation and the clouds forming in a dramatic sky. This vivid imagery makes the concept more engaging and easier to recall.

Another technique is to use mind maps or diagrams, where you sketch out the relationships between ideas. This helps organize information visually and allows you to see connections that might not be immediately obvious in a text-based format.

Scenarios where visualization enhances memory are numerous. Consider a student preparing for an exam on human anatomy. By visualizing the body as a complex network of interconnected systems, they can picture how blood flows through veins, how muscles contract, or how nerves transmit signals. This mental imagery provides a framework that helps to understand and recall during the test. Similarly, when planning a project, visualizing the sequence of tasks as a flow chart can help you remember the order and dependencies of each step. Imagery acts as a mental anchor, making it easier to retrieve information when needed.

Incorporating visualization into your daily routine can have lasting benefits for memory improvement. One way to do this is by visualizing daily tasks or goals during your morning routine. As you sip your coffee, imagine your day unfolding like a storyboard, each task a scene that leads naturally to the next. This practice helps you organize your day and primes your mind for action.

Meditation or relaxation techniques can also enhance visualization skills. During a quiet moment, allow your mind to wander through a mental scene, focusing on the sights, sounds and feelings. This exercise not only relaxes the mind but also sharpens your ability to create and retain detailed mental images.

Visualization is more than just a memory aid; creating vivid images transforms abstract ideas into something tangible and memorable. This effective and enjoyable technique encourages you to explore your imagination and creativity. As you practice visualization regularly, you'll find that your ability to recall information improves, making learning and memory retention more intuitive and effective.

Memory Palace Journey Description

Imagine you're entering a spacious, contemporary house for a memorable journey through its various rooms, each distinctly decorated and filled with unique objects to aid in your memory exercise.

The Hallway: As you open the bright red front door, you're greeted by a large ornate mirror to your right and a small, antique wooden table to your left. On the table sits a silver tray holding a set of keys and a white porcelain vase with fresh red roses.

The Living Room: Moving forward into the living room, you see a deep blue sofa facing a stone fireplace where a brass clock ticks prominently on the mantel. Adjacent to the fireplace is a tall bookshelf filled with assorted books, a model ship and a globe.

The Kitchen: Next, you enter the kitchen, where a round table covered with a checkered tablecloth stands in the center. There's a fruit bowl filled with bananas and apples on the table. Hanging above the table is a chandelier with crystal pendants. The counter holds a red coffee maker and a stack of green plates.

The Study: Heading into the study, you notice a large oak desk dominating the room, with a black leather chair pushed against it. There are several items on the desk: a laptop, a stack of colorful notebooks and a brass desk lamp. The wall above the desk features an array of family photos.

The Bedroom: Lastly, the bedroom features a king-sized bed with navy blue bedding and gold pillows. A plush grey rug lies at the foot of the bed and beside it stands a nightstand on which rests a digital alarm clock and a stack of three mystery novels.

Memory Palace Quiz

Now, test your recall of the details from each room in the memory palace:

The Hallway: What color is the front door and what items are placed on the antique table?

Living Room: Describe two items found on the mantel of the fireplace and one item from the bookshelf.

Kitchen: What are the two main colors noticed in the kitchen and what items can be found on the round table?

Study: What are the three items located on the oak desk and what decorates the wall above it?

Bedroom: What are the colors of the bedding?

10

Cultural Sensitivity in Communication

"Cultural diversity brings a collective strength that can benefit all."
Robert Allan

In a conference room filled with professionals from around the globe, a simple gesture—a nod, a smile, a handshake—can carry different meanings, each shaped by cultural diversity. These small actions, often taken for granted, can bridge or widen gaps, depending on our awareness and sensitivity.

Cultural diversity in communication isn't just about avoiding faux pas; it's about embracing the wealth of perspectives that different backgrounds bring. When diverse teams come together, they don't just share ideas; they create a synergy that can lead to unprecedented innovation. I've seen many creative solutions emerge when people from varied backgrounds collaborate, each bringing unique insights shaped by their experiences and cultures. This blend of perspectives fosters an environment where new ideas flourish, challenging conventional thinking and pushing boundaries.

Consider the benefits of cultural insights in problem-solving. When a team comprises individuals from different cultures, they're equipped to approach challenges from multiple angles. This diversity of thought can lead to more comprehensive solutions. It's like having a kit with various tools, each suited for a specific task. Studies have shown that a workplace that embraces cultural diversity can lead to better decision-making and a more inclusive environment where everyone feels valued[6]. This inclusivity doesn't just transform the dynamics within teams; it also opens doors to wider markets and audiences, reflecting the diversity of the world we live in.

Solving Complex Problems in a Multicultural Team

A few years ago, I was coaching a team leader of a multinational NGO. He was responsible for co-ordinating a complex project involving team members from Brazil, Sweden and India. The aim was to launch a health initiative in multiple countries. He confided in me that the team faced communication challenges and conflicts over project management styles. The Swedish members preferred a more egalitarian and direct approach, while the Brazilian and Indian members were accustomed to a more hierarchical structure and indirect communication. So here's what we did.

- **Workshops:** We ran several cross-cultural workshops to help team members understand each other's communication styles and work preferences.

- **Facilitation:** A facilitator was brought in to help mediate discussions, ensuring that all cultural perspectives were respected and understood.

- **Hybrid Approaches:** The team adopted a hybrid management approach, blending direct and indirect communication and respecting hierarchical sensitivities without compromising egalitarian values.

- **Outcome:** This culturally sensitive approach allowed the team to collaborate more effectively, leveraging the diverse strengths of its members. The health initiative was successfully launched with tailored approaches in each target country, reflecting the nuanced understanding of local contexts contributed by team members.

Be Open & Curious

To truly appreciate and understand different cultures, it's crucial to approach them with a mindset of openness and curiosity. This means actively seeking knowledge and experiences that broaden your understanding of cultures other than your own. Participating in cultural events and festivals is one way to immerse yourself in the traditions and practices of different communities. These experiences offer a firsthand glimpse into the values and customs that shape people's lives, providing a richer context for your interactions.

I find that reading literature and watching films from various cultures transports me to different worlds, offering narratives and perspectives that deepen my empathy and understanding. These stories are windows into the lives and experiences of others, allowing me to connect with them on a more profound level.

Asking respectful questions invites others to share their cultural stories and insights. For instance, instead of making assumptions about a colleague's background, you might ask, "What are some traditions you celebrate with your family?" or "How do you find this cultural practice impacts your daily life?" These questions demonstrate your interest and create a space for cultural exchange.

Integrating diverse perspectives into conversations and decision-making processes requires intentional effort and openness. One effective strategy is to foster inclusive brainstorming sessions where every voice is heard and valued. Encourage team members to share their ideas and insights, ensuring that each perspective is considered in the decision-making process. This might involve setting ground rules that promote equal participation, such as rotating speaking turns or using anonymous idea submissions to ensure everyone feels comfortable contributing.

Take a moment to reflect on a recent conversation where cultural differences were present. Consider the questions you asked and the responses you received. How did curiosity shape the interaction? Jot down a few questions you might ask in future encounters to deepen your understanding and connection. Reflect on how these questions can foster a more inclusive and culturally sensitive dialogue.

Recognizing and Respecting Cultural Norms

Cultural norms are the unwritten rules that guide behavior within a society. They shape how we greet one another, how we express respect and even how we communicate. These norms influence expectations and interactions, often without us realizing it. For instance, in Japan, bowing is a common greeting, a gesture deeply rooted in respect and tradition. Meanwhile, a handshake is the norm in Western cultures, symbolizing openness and equality. Understanding these customs goes beyond mere etiquette; it is about recognizing the values they represent. In many Asian cultures, hierarchical respect is crucial, dictating how individuals interact based on age or status. Ignoring such norms can lead to misunderstandings, affecting social and business relationships. In professional settings, recognizing these nuances can mean the difference between a successful negotiation and a missed opportunity.

When entering a new cultural setting, take time to observe social interactions. Watch how locals greet each other, note the language they use, and pay attention to their body language. This silent observation can offer invaluable insights into the standards that guide their interactions. Additionally, seeking guidance from cultural insiders or mentors can be incredibly helpful. These individuals provide context and explanations that deepen your understanding. They offer perspectives that might not be immediately visible, helping you navigate the nuances of a new culture with greater ease. By actively listening to their experiences and advice, you can better adapt to and respect the cultural norms of those around you.

Respecting cultural differences is foundational in building trust and fostering positive relationships. It demonstrates an appreciation for the values and traditions of others, creating a sense of mutual respect.

In business negotiations, for example, acknowledging and adhering to cultural norms can significantly impact outcomes. Respect for hierarchy, understanding the importance of saving face, and adapting communication styles to suit cultural expectations are just a few ways respect can enhance negotiations. Ignoring these norms, however, can lead to misunderstandings.

Imagine a meeting where a Western executive addresses a Middle Eastern counterpart by their first name without prior permission. In many Middle Eastern cultures, such personal familiarity in a formal business setting may be seen as presumptuous or disrespectful. This cultural faux pas could make the counterpart feel undervalued or disrespected, potentially compromising the relationship and obstructing successful negotiations. This small oversight can derail the conversation, creating tension and hindering collaboration.

Diplomats often undergo extensive cultural training, honing their skills to navigate diverse cultural landscapes with sensitivity and respect. This preparation allows them to communicate effectively, even when cultural norms differ drastically.

Cross-cultural friendships also thrive on respect for each other's backgrounds. Take, for instance, a friendship between an American and an Indian. By respecting each other's customs—whether it be celebrating Diwali or acknowledging the importance of Thanksgiving—the friendship deepens. These relationships are built on an understanding that transcends cultural differences, fostering an enriched and resilient connection.

In our world of interconnectedness, embracing cultural norms is more crucial than ever. It requires a willingness to step outside of comfort zones and explore the vast array of human experiences that cultures offer. By doing so, you show respect and gain a deeper appreciation for the diversity that shapes our world. This respect is not just about avoiding missteps; it's about building bridges and creating spaces where varied perspectives can flourish. As you navigate these different relationships, remember that the goal is not to perfect every interaction but to approach each with openness and a genuine desire to connect.

Adapting Communication Styles for Cultural Sensitivity

Imagine you're attending a business meeting with colleagues from different corners of the globe. As the discussion unfolds, you notice that what seems to be effective communication for one person might not work for another. This difference often stems from the varying communication styles inherent in different cultures. Understanding the need to adapt your communication style is crucial when interacting across cultures.

Some cultures, known as high context, rely heavily on implicit communication and non-verbal cues. In these settings, much is understood through context, relationships and shared experiences. Japan and many Middle Eastern countries exemplify high-context communication, where messages are often indirect and understanding the subtleties is key.

Conversely, low-context cultures, like the United States and Germany, prioritize explicit, direct communication. Clarity and detail are valued in these environments, with less reliance on the surrounding context to convey meaning. See the table at the end of this chapter.

Furthermore, the preference for direct versus indirect communication varies across cultures. Direct communication is straightforward and unambiguous, often favored in low-context cultures where honesty and clarity are paramount. In contrast, indirect communication is more nuanced, focusing on maintaining harmony and avoiding confrontation. This style is prevalent in high-context cultures, where the relationship takes precedence over bluntness. Recognizing these differences can help you navigate conversations with cultural sensitivity, adjusting your approach to align with the preferences of those you interact with.

Adapting your communication style involves practical strategies that align with cultural expectations. One technique is adjusting your tone and formality based on the cultural context. In some cultures, a formal tone is a sign of respect, particularly in professional settings. This might mean using titles and honorifics or maintaining a certain level of politeness in your language. In more relaxed cultures, informal language might be more appropriate, fostering a sense of camaraderie and openness.

Additionally, when communicating in low-context cultures, strive for clarity by using concise language. Avoid jargon or idiomatic expressions that might not translate well, ensuring your message is understood without relying on context. This approach not only enhances understanding but also demonstrates respect for the communication preferences of your audience.

Adapting communication styles can present challenges, particularly when balancing authenticity with respect for cultural differences. You might find yourself navigating the fine line between staying true to your personality and adjusting to fit the cultural norms of others. The key is maintaining clarity while adapting your style, ensuring your message is not lost in translation. This requires a delicate balance, where you honor the cultural context without sacrificing authenticity. It's important to approach these challenges with an open mind and be willing to learn and adapt as needed. This flexibility enhances your communication and fosters mutual respect and understanding.

Consider engaging in exercises that encourage adaptation to become more flexible in your communication approaches. Role-playing scenarios with diverse cultural contexts can be particularly effective. This involves practicing conversations with individuals from different backgrounds and experimenting with various communication styles to see what resonates. These exercises provide a safe space to explore and refine your approach, offering insights into how different styles impact interactions. Reflective exercises on past cross-cultural interactions can also be valuable. By analyzing previous experiences, you can identify what worked well and where adjustments might be needed. This reflection encourages continuous learning and growth, empowering you to adapt your communication style with confidence and ease.

Avoiding Cultural Missteps in Dialogue

Picture yourself at an international business meeting. You're feeling confident and ready to make a great impression. But in an instant, a seemingly harmless gesture causes the room to fall silent. You've unknowingly committed a cultural blunder. Misinterpretations of gestures and body language are among the most common oversights that derail communication. For instance, a thumbs-up might be a positive affirmation in one culture, but in another, it can be offensive. Similarly, eye contact, a sign of engagement in some societies, might be seen as disrespectful in others. These unintentional missteps can create barriers, impacting relationships and causing unnecessary tension.

Language, too, can be a minefield. Words and phrases that seem neutral to us might carry unintended meanings elsewhere. For example, colloquial expressions or idioms that translate poorly can confuse or offend. Even the tone of voice can alter the message. What sounds assertive in one language may come off as aggressive in another. These language-related pitfalls require careful navigation to prevent misunderstandings that might compromise your intentions. The consequences of such missteps can be significant, leading to damaged relationships, lost opportunities and a communication breakdown.

To avoid these cultural pitfalls, preparation is paramount. Before engaging in cross-cultural interactions, take the time to research the cultural etiquette of the people you'll be communicating with. This might involve learning about their customs, traditions and social norms. Understanding the historical and cultural context can explain why certain gestures or words are significant. Seeking feedback from cultural liaisons or colleagues familiar with the culture can also be invaluable. They can offer guidance, helping you navigate the intricacies of communication that might take time to become apparent.

In a cultural misstep, humility and the ability to apologize can make a significant difference. Acknowledging mistakes openly, without defensiveness, shows respect and a willingness to learn. A sincere apology can go a long way in repairing any damage caused by cultural blunders. It's about accepting responsibility and expressing a genuine desire to understand and improve. Consider the impact of a thoughtful apology that acknowledges the error and seeks to learn from it. Such gestures can restore harmony, demonstrating that your intentions were never to offend.

Many apologies have mended relationships and fostered greater understanding between different cultures.

In 2008, the Australian government formally apologized to the indigenous Aboriginal population for past injustices, including the forced removal of children from their families. This apology, delivered by then Prime Minister Kevin Rudd, was a landmark in Australian history and marked a step towards reconciliation and better understanding between the Indigenous communities and the broader Australian society.

In 2018, Dolce & Gabbana faced backlash for an advertising campaign perceived as stereotyping and disrespecting Chinese culture. The founders, Domenico Dolce and Stefano Gabbana issued a video apology in Mandarin, acknowledging their mistake and expressing their love and respect for Chinese culture. This apology was important in mending the relationship with Chinese consumers and demonstrating cultural sensitivity.

Continuous learning and adaptation are crucial for navigating the complexities of cross-cultural communication. Each interaction offers an opportunity for growth, allowing you to refine your understanding and approach. Embracing a mindset of cultural learning means being open to new experiences and willing to adapt. It involves celebrating small successes in cultural sensitivity and recognizing that each step forward enhances your communication ability. This learning journey is ongoing, requiring patience and a commitment to personal growth. You pave the way for more meaningful and enriching connections by approaching cultural interactions with curiosity and openness.

As we conclude this chapter, remember that cultural sensitivity is not an end point but a continuous process of learning and adapting. It's about recognizing the richness diverse perspectives bring to our lives and communication. Let this be the beginning of your exploration into the intricate world of cultural dialogue, where every conversation is an opportunity to deepen your understanding and broaden your horizons.

This table compares high-context and low-context cultures along with specific communication strategies that are effective in each. It illustrates the differences and shows how to adapt your communication approach accordingly.

Communication Strategies for Each CultureType:

High-Context Cultures: Japan, Arab, China

- **Prioritize Relationship Building:**
  Spend time building relationships before getting into business or negotiations.

- **Observe Non-verbal Cues:**
  Pay attention to body language, tone of voice, and facial expressions, as they are integral to understanding the entire message.

- **Use Indirect Language:**
  Be sensitive to the indirect communication style, using tact and reading between the lines.

- **Seek to Understand the Context:**
  Understand the background and the environment your counterparts are operating within to better interpret their communications.

Low-Context Cultures: USA, Germany, Scandanavia

- **Be Clear and Concise:**
  Communicate your ideas clearly and avoid ambiguity as these cultures value straightforwardness.

- **Focus on the Task:**
  Emphasize getting to the point and dealing with tasks directly.

- **Use Direct Questions:**
  Feel free to ask direct questions to clarify points and make sure mutual understanding is achieved.

- **Provide Detailed Explanations:**
  Do not rely on shared background or knowledge; explain with specifics and details as needed.

11

Special Considerations for Introverts

"Quiet people have the loudest minds." Stephen Hawkings

Leveraging Introverted Strengths in Conversations

Bill Gates is often described as an introvert. Despite being one of the richest individuals in the world and a leading figure in technology and philanthropy, Gates has frequently shared in interviews and his writings that he is naturally introverted. He is known for his deep focus and concentration, a common trait among introverts. This ability allowed him to spend hours coding and solving complex problems during the early days of Microsoft, driving innovation and setting the stage for the technology revolution.

Gates is not known for being outspoken or charismatic in the traditional, extroverted sense. Instead, he communicates thoughtfully and deliberately. He has used his platform to advocate for global health and education reforms, influencing policy and public opinion through well-reasoned arguments and detailed presentations. Instead of relying on charisma, Gates led Microsoft with a focus on strategic planning and execution. His reflective and analytical leadership style helped Microsoft innovate and remain a leader in competitive tech spaces.

He has also used his introverted nature in public advocacy, often sharing detailed research and data to make compelling arguments for his causes.

He regularly thoughtfully engages with leaders and experts, facilitating discussions that lead to actionable insights and solutions.

I share this with you because Bill Gates exemplifies how introverts can leverage their natural tendencies towards deep thought, concentration, and careful planning to effect positive change on a global scale. His work has not only transformed the technology landscape but also significantly contributed to improving health and education outcomes worldwide.

Through my work, I have learned that introverts have an innate ability to listen deeply, which fosters genuine understanding and connection. While extroverts might enthusiastically dominate a conversation, introverts excel in creating space for others to express themselves. This ability to listen attentively allows you to pick up on subtle cues and emotions, offering insights that others might overlook. Your thoughtful nature means that when you do speak, your words carry weight and depth. By embracing these qualities, you can transform conversations, making them more meaningful and impactful.

Introverts often take time to consider their words carefully. This introspection results in well-considered opinions and questions that add depth to discussions. Before entering a conversation, some find preparing topics or questions of interest helpful. This preparation boosts confidence and ensures that your contributions are insightful and relevant.

Introverts need to consider strategies that highlight their contributions to ensure their voice is heard and appreciated in group settings. Volunteering to lead or organize small group discussions can provide a platform to share your ideas in a controlled environment. Your natural leadership and listening skills can shine in these settings as you guide the conversation with empathy and focus. Additionally, writing follow-up emails is a powerful tool for introverts. When thoughts go unvoiced in meetings, an articulate email can capture your insights and ensure they're acknowledged and valued. This approach allows you to contribute meaningfully without the pressure of on-the-spot speaking.

One-on-one conversations are where introverts often truly excel. In these intimate settings, you have the opportunity to engage deeply with individuals, free from the distractions of larger groups. Small meetings can often be more productive than large gatherings.

Here are some tips to enhance one-on-one interactions:

- **Choose the right setting:**
  Opt for quiet, comfortable environments where you can focus without distractions. A cozy café or a serene park can be ideal.

- **Prepare thoughtful questions:**
  Before the meeting, consider questions that invite deeper dialogue. This preparation will help guide the conversation and ensure it remains engaging.

- **Be present:**
  During the conversation, practice active listening. Pay attention to verbal and non-verbal cues, and respond thoughtfully, reinforcing your interest and understanding.

- **Reflect and follow up:**
  After the meeting, take a moment to reflect on the conversation. Consider sending a follow-up message expressing gratitude and summarizing key points discussed. This gesture reinforces your connection and leaves a lasting impression.

Preparing for Social Engagements with Intention

Walking into a social event can feel like stepping onto a stage, lights glaring, and the audience waiting. For introverts, this can be daunting. To navigate these situations with confidence, setting clear objectives can really help. Before attending an event, take a moment to identify your specific networking goals. Are you aiming to meet a certain number of new contacts, or is there a particular individual you'd like to connect with?

These objectives provide focus and direction, turning what might feel like a chaotic whirlwind into a series of achievable tasks. This intention acts as your compass, guiding your interactions and ensuring each conversation feels purposeful rather than perfunctory.

Beyond setting goals, preparing your mindset and emotions is crucial. Visualization exercises can be particularly effective here. Picture yourself at the event, engaging in successful conversations, feeling at ease and connected. This mental rehearsal can ease anxiety, replacing fear with familiarity. Similarly, affirmations can bolster your confidence. Simple phrases like "I am capable of meaningful conversations" or "I bring value to every interaction" can shift your mindset, reducing self-doubt. By affirming your strengths, you step into the event with a sense of empowerment, ready to embrace new encounters.

Pre-event research and planning are often overlooked but are powerful strategies. Knowing who will be attending or speaking can be a game-changer. You can identify common interests or professional overlaps by researching attendees and providing natural conversation starters. Planning conversation topics related to the event theme can further enhance your preparedness. These small acts of research create a sense of familiarity, transforming the unknown into the known and allowing you to approach conversations with curiosity and confidence.

Personal rituals can serve as grounding anchors in the moments leading up to an event. Establish a routine that calms your mind and centers your focus. As mentioned in previous chapters, deep breathing exercises can be incredibly effective; they slow your heart rate and help you remain present. As you breathe in, visualize positive energy filling your body, and as you exhale, imagine stress and anxiety leaving your body. This simple practice can have a profound impact on your state of mind. Listening to calming music or podcasts en-route to the event can also set a positive tone. Choose content that inspires or soothes you, creating a mental space where you feel relaxed and open to new experiences.

Creating Personal Conversation Comfort Zones

For many introverts, walking into a room that's buzzing with chatter and laughter can feel like stepping into a foreign land, where the noise and energy levels are overwhelming. To navigate these spaces with ease, consider the concept of conversation comfort zones—environments that feel familiar and reassuring, allowing you to engage more naturally. Choosing venues that are comforting can make a world of difference, these settings provide a sense of control, enabling you to focus on the conversation rather than the chaos around you. Physical spaces that allow for quieter interactions are particularly beneficial, as they reduce sensory overload and create a more intimate atmosphere. In these environments, you can connect more deeply without the distraction of background noise or bustling crowds.

Establishing conversational boundaries within these comfort zones is equally important. It's about knowing your limits and respecting them to protect your energy. If you feel overwhelmed, it's perfectly acceptable to excuse yourself politely. A simple "I need a moment to recharge" can be both respectful and practical. Scheduling breaks during long events is another strategy to help maintain your energy levels. Stepping outside for a few minutes of fresh air or finding a quiet space, to regroup can provide the solitude needed to refresh and return with renewed focus. By setting these boundaries, you honor your needs, ensuring that each social interaction is enjoyable and sustainable. You will be surprised to discover that most people will respect your honesty and the opportunity to recharge their own social battery.

The presence of trusted allies in your comfort zones can offer invaluable support. Attending events with a friend or colleague who understands your preferences can alleviate much of the pressure. They can help navigate conversations, introduce you to new people, or provide familiarity in an unfamiliar setting. Having someone by your side who knows when to step in or when to step back can make social engagements feel less daunting. Partnering with someone who shares your social rhythm can transform even the most intimidating environments into welcoming spaces.

Personalizing your comfort zones to fit your preferences can enhance your social experiences. Bringing personal items that provide comfort—like a favorite pen or notebook—can offer reassurance. These items serve as reference points, grounding you when interactions become too much. Positioning yourself in quieter areas of a venue can also help. Whether choosing a table away from the main crowd or sitting near an exit, these minor adjustments can create a buffer, allowing you to engage at your own pace. Tailoring your environment in these ways makes you feel more at ease and empowers you to participate fully and authentically in conversations.

People have told me that these strategies have helped transform social engagements from draining obligations into opportunities for genuine interaction.

Strategies for Sustainable Social Energy

Recognizing the signs of social fatigue is the first step in managing your energy. When you start to feel drained, it often manifests as a sense of irritability or an overwhelming urge to withdraw. These are signals from your body and mind that it's time for a break. Ignoring them can lead to burnout, making future interactions even more challenging. Balancing social activities with periods of solitude is essential. Just as athletes need rest days to recover and build strength, introverts need downtime to recharge. This balance lets you approach social engagements with renewed vigor and enthusiasm rather than dread.

The role of prioritization in managing social energy cannot be overstated. Choosing social engagements that align with your personal goals and values is vital. Not every invitation needs a "yes." Select events that offer personal or professional growth opportunities. These are the interactions that will nourish you, providing more than just surface-level connections.

Conversely, learn to decline invitations that don't resonate with your interests. It's about quality, not quantity. By focusing your energy on interactions that matter, you ensure that you're investing your time and resources wisely. This selective approach allows you to maintain your energy reserves for the moments that count.

Self-reflection is a powerful tool in understanding your energy patterns. I encourage you to keep a journal and track your high and low energy periods, providing insights into your social rhythms. Reflect on past engagements to determine when you felt most energized and when you didn't. Was it the environment, the people, or perhaps the time of day? Identifying these factors can guide you in planning future interactions, allowing you to choose the best times and settings for socializing. This awareness empowers you to tailor your social calendar to fit your energy needs, ensuring you remain vibrant and engaged in your interactions.

Managing your energy effectively will not only improve your communication skills but enhance your overall well-being. Engaging meaningfully without feeling depleted is a gift that keeps giving, enriching your personal and professional relationships. As you continue this journey, remember that your energy is valuable. Treat it with the care and respect it deserves, and it will serve you well.

Social Personality Quiz: Are You an Introvert or an Extrovert?

Answer each question truthfully based on how you typically feel or behave in social situations. At the end, count the number of A's, B's, and C's to see if you're more of an introvert or an extrovert.

When you go to a party with lots of new people, you usually:

A) Stick to your close friends and avoid initiating conversations with strangers.

B) Sometimes mix between sticking with friends and meeting new people.

C) Enjoy meeting new people and often start conversations with strangers.

How do you feel after spending a few hours surrounded by a lot of people?

A) Drained, and you need time alone to recharge.

B) It depends on the context and the people involved.

C) Energized and ready for more social interaction.

If you had to choose, what kind of vacation would you prefer?

A) A quiet retreat in a secluded place with a few close friends or family members.

B) A balanced vacation with some days spent in solitude and other days exploring busy tourist spots.

C) A bustling city trip with lots of activities and social opportunities.

When it comes to making new friends, you:

A) Find it quite challenging and prefer to have a few close friends.

B) Can sometimes find it easy, but other times you're hesitant.

C) Find it easy and enjoyable to expand your social circle.

At work or in class, when you have a big project, you prefer to:

A) Work alone, as it's easier to concentrate and function effectively.

B) Work alone or with others, depending on the nature of the project.

C) Work in a team, as the interaction stimulates your creativity.

During conversations, you:

A) Tend to listen more and speak less.

B) Balance listening and talking, depending on who you're with.

C) Tend to dominate the conversation and share your thoughts freely.

How do you usually feel about talking on the phone or video calls?

A) Avoid it if possible, preferring texts or emails instead.

B) Don't mind it sometimes, but it's not always your favorite.

C) Enjoy it and often spend a long time chatting away.

You're more likely to spend your free evening:

A) Reading a book or engaging in a hobby at home alone.

B) Maybe catching up with a friend or two or just relaxing at home.

C) Going out to social events or inviting friends over.

How do you usually handle conflict in social or work situations?

A) Prefer to deal with it internally or avoid confrontation.

B) Address it if necessary, but it's not your comfort zone.

C) Tackle it head-on, discussing issues openly with all parties involved.

What is your approach to social media?

A) Limited use, mainly to keep in touch with close friends and family.

B) You use it moderately, depending on your mood and purpose.

C) Very active, enjoy engaging with many people and making new connections.

Results:

Mostly A's: Introvert —You likely find social interactions with strangers or large groups draining and prefer more intimate gatherings or alone time.

Mostly B's: Ambivert —You exhibit traits of both introverts and extroverts, depending on the situation. You can enjoy social interaction but also value your alone time.

Mostly C's: Extrovert —You thrive in social situations and feel energized by interacting with others, including strangers.

This quiz offers a general look into where you might fall on the introversion-extroversion spectrum in social contexts. Remember, personality can be fluid, and people may exhibit different traits in different situations.

12

Advanced Psychological Insights

"Seek first to understand, then to be understood." St Francis of Assisi

Do you sometimes feel judged as soon as you walk into a room of strangers? Do you find yourself judging others before you've even started to talk to them? Most of us do. It's part of human nature. A series of experiments[7] by Princeton psychologists Janine Willis and Alexander Todorov show that we form an impression of a stranger from their face, often within milliseconds, and this first impression tends to influence all future interactions.

This phenomenon is known as the primacy effect, where the information we first encounter about someone heavily impacts our ongoing perceptions. It's why those first few moments matter so profoundly.

First Impressions

First impressions hinge on a complex interplay of visual cues and body language. Your posture, facial expressions, and even the tilt of your head can communicate volumes without uttering a sound. As mentioned in the chapter about body language, a confident stance and a warm smile can convey approachability, while crossed arms and averted eyes might suggest aloofness or discomfort. These non-verbal signals are potent, as they tap into our primal instincts, influencing how others perceive us. In professional settings, attire and grooming add another layer to these impressions. The clothes you choose and how you present yourself can speak to your personality competence and attention to detail, subtly guiding the opinions others form about you. A friend of mine who advocates for women's empowerment, uses her wardrobe to echo that message. She always wears pink tops or jackets, dyes her hair pink, and wears spectacles with pink frames. What are you conveying through your appearance?

Crafting a positive first impression involves more than what you wear; it's about the energy you project. It's about finding that sweet spot between confidence and warmth. Your language, both verbal and non-verbal, plays a crucial role.

Choosing words that reflect positivity and maintaining an approachable demeanor can make you seem more inviting. These elements, when harmonized, create a memorable first impression that can open doors and foster positive connections. Despite our best efforts, sometimes first impressions falter. Perhaps you were distracted or nervous, and the interaction didn't unfold as you hoped. I remember a client of mine, Ethan, telling me he was excited yet nervous about attending a high-profile networking event in his industry. It was his first big opportunity to make connections that could advance his career. He spent the week before the event brushing up on industry news, preparing an elevator pitch and picking a professional outfit.

On the evening of the event, Ethan arrived at the venue, a sleek hotel, he checked in, grabbed a name badge and stepped into the grand ballroom filled with professionals exchanging business cards. The atmosphere was charged with opportunity, and Ethan felt a surge of confidence. However, as he approached a group of potential contacts, his phone vibrated intensely in his pocket. It was an urgent work call that couldn't be ignored, so he stepped outside to respond, thinking it would only take a moment.

Unfortunately, sorting out the issue took longer than expected, and by the time he returned the group had dispersed.

Attempting to regroup, Ethan told me that he approached another cluster of attendees. He introduced himself with a smile and reached out for a handshake. As he did, he accidentally knocked the other person's drink. The spill was minor, but it was enough to fluster Ethan and divert the conversation toward apologies and cleanup rather than business and opportunities. Despite the rocky start, Ethan laughed off the mishap, which helped break the ice. The rest of the evening went smoother, with Ethan making a few good connections, although not as many as he had hoped. He left the event with mixed feelings—grateful for the contacts he made but aware that his first impressions might not have been as impactful as intended due to distractions and a bit of bad luck.

The good news is that negative first impressions, while sticky, are not set in stone. Acknowledging any missteps openly and sincerely can be a decisive first step in repairing them. Demonstrating consistent positive behavior over time can gradually reshape perceptions. Actions speak louder than words, and by consistently showing up in a positive light, you can gradually overwrite initial judgments.

First Impression Exercises

Engage in role-playing with a friend or colleague where you practice introductions. Focus on refining your body language, tone, and choice of words to create a welcoming atmosphere. Observe how these changes impact your friend's perception and gather feedback. Additionally, observe others in social settings or through video analysis. Note the elements contributing to strong first impressions and consider how you might incorporate similar techniques into your interactions. This practice will help hone your skills, making those pivotal first moments more impactful.

Understanding the art of first impressions equips you with the tools to gracefully navigate social and professional environments. By harnessing the power of visual cues, body language, and genuine self-presentation, you can create the impressions you wish to leave on others.

Using Persuasion Techniques Ethically

I remember the first time I truly understood the power of persuasion. During a community meeting, a local leader spoke passionately to create change. He didn't manipulate the audience or twist the truth. Instead, he laid out his vision with transparency and honesty, respecting the intelligence and autonomy of those he addressed. This approach is the cornerstone of ethical persuasion: building trust through sincerity and shared goals rather than coercion or deceit. Moral persuasion is about aligning your intentions with the needs and values of your audience, ensuring mutual benefit and respect.

Persuasion becomes ethical when it is rooted in transparency. This means being upfront about your intentions and providing truthful information. It's about engaging others with respect, valuing their perspectives, and recognizing their right to make informed decisions. Ethical persuasion also involves crafting logical arguments supported by evidence, creating a foundation of credibility and trust. When you present data or anecdotes, ensure they are accurate and relevant, reinforcing the integrity of your message. Highlighting shared values and goals can further strengthen your persuasive efforts. By aligning your objectives with those of your audience, you create a sense of partnership and common purpose, making your message more compelling.

The impact of ethical persuasion on relationships can be profound. When you persuade with integrity, you lay the groundwork for long-term partnerships built on trust and cooperation. Consider a negotiation scenario where both parties enter with a clear understanding of their respective goals and constraints. They foster a collaborative atmosphere that enhances mutual respect and trust by maintaining openness and seeking win-win outcomes. This approach resolves immediate issues and strengthens the relationship, paving the way for future cooperation.

In team settings, persuasive communication can enhance collaboration by encouraging open dialogue and shared decision-making, ultimately leading to more effective and innovative outcomes.

There are countless examples of ethical persuasion in practice that demonstrate its positive impact. I recall a case where a company I worked with sought to merge with a smaller firm. Rather than using aggressive tactics, the larger company presented a vision for the merger that emphasized the benefits for both parties, such as increased market reach and shared resources. By focusing on transparency and mutual gain, they secured a fair and beneficial deal, setting the stage for a successful partnership.

Nelson Mandela, once a political prisoner for 27 years under the apartheid regime, became the first Black President of South Africa in 1994. His leadership was pivotal during the fragile transition from an apartheid state to a democracy. Mandela's approach to leadership and reconciliation was grounded in ethical persuasion, focusing on unity, forgiveness, and inclusivity. One of his most striking acts was his support for the South African national rugby team, the Springboks, during the 1995 Rugby World Cup. Previously, the Springboks had been a symbol of white oppression. However, Mandela embraced the team and encouraged all South Africans to do the same, which helped bridge racial divides and foster a sense of national unity. This act was not just symbolic but a deliberate, strategic effort to bring a divided country together and heal the wounds of apartheid. Mandela's leadership and his ethical approach to persuasion helped to stabilize a volatile political landscape and lay the foundation for the peaceful coexistence of diverse racial groups in South Africa. Mandela's example demonstrates how ethical persuasion can be used effectively to promote peace and reconciliation, highlighting its positive impact on a national and even global scale.

Incorporating the principles of ethical persuasion into your daily interactions can transform how you communicate and connect with others. By focusing on transparency, respect, and shared goals, you enhance your ability to persuade and build stronger, more meaningful relationships. Whether in professional settings, community initiatives, or personal interactions, ethical persuasion is a powerful tool for fostering trust, cooperation, and positive change.

Understanding Group Dynamics in Conversations

Group dynamics stand out in human interaction as a vibrant, complex pattern. Unlike one-on-one conversations, group settings introduce many social roles and hierarchies. Each participant brings a unique voice, yet they often navigate unspoken rules that govern the interaction. Social roles can dictate who speaks the most and whose opinions are given the most weight. Formal or informal hierarchies can influence the flow of conversation, often determining who leads and who follows. These dynamics are crucial to understanding, affecting how ideas are shared, and decisions are made. The size of the group also plays a significant role. In a smaller group, each voice might have more space to be heard, while in a larger gathering, some might find themselves lost in the crowd. This can impact communication flow, creating a need for strategies that ensure everyone has a chance to participate.

Navigating group conversations effectively requires awareness and adaptability. Techniques for facilitating inclusive dialogue are key. Encouraging everyone to contribute can be as simple as inviting quieter participants to share their thoughts. This might involve directly asking them for their opinions or creating an environment where they feel comfortable speaking up. As mentioned in chapter six, managing dominant voices is another challenge. While some individuals naturally take charge, their dominance can stifle others. One way to balance this is by setting ground rules at the start of the discussion, such as limiting how long one person can speak or rotating the speaking order. This ensures that all voices are heard, promoting a more balanced and equitable conversation. Encouraging quieter participants to voice their opinions can also be facilitated by breaking the group into smaller units or using technology like chat functions for anonymous input.

Groupthink and conformity pose significant challenges in group settings. Groupthink occurs when the desire for harmony or conformity results in irrational or dysfunctional decision-making. It can suppress dissenting viewpoints and stifle creativity. To counter this, it's important to foster an environment where diverse opinions are encouraged and valued. Encouraging critical thinking involves asking probing questions and challenging assumptions. Facilitators can play a crucial role by actively seeking alternative perspectives and highlighting their importance to the group. Creating a culture where dissent is respected requires patience and a commitment to openness. It might mean explicitly stating that all ideas are welcome and that disagreement is a natural part of the process. This can prevent the silencing of minority opinions and help avoid the pitfalls of groupthink.

Practicing Group Communication Skills

Consider participating in group debates focusing on balanced contributions to refine your group communication skills. This involves setting a topic and dividing it into smaller groups, where each person is responsible for presenting a point of view. Role-playing scenarios can also be beneficial. Practice leading group discussions by taking turns facilitating and managing the conversation. This exercise helps develop skills in guiding dialogue, encouraging participation, and managing group dynamics. As you engage in these practices, pay close attention to the flow of conversation and the balance of voices. Reflect on your experiences and consider what strategies worked well and where improvements could be made.

Understanding and navigating group dynamics is not just about managing the conversation; it's about fostering an environment where all participants feel valued and heard. By employing strategies that promote inclusivity and critical thinking, you can enhance your ability to engage effectively in group settings. These skills are valuable in professional contexts and enrich personal interactions, allowing for more meaningful and productive exchanges.

The Role of Cognitive Biases in Communication

Think about the moment you form an opinion of someone based on a single interaction. This is the power of cognitive biases at play. Cognitive biases are systematic patterns of deviation from norm or rationality in judgment, affecting how we perceive and interact with others. These biases can warp our understanding, leading us to make judgments that may not always be fair or accurate.

Take confirmation bias, for instance, where we tend to seek information that confirms our pre-existing beliefs, ignoring evidence to the contrary. This bias can create echo chambers, reinforcing our views without challenging them.

Similarly, the halo effect idealizes someone based on one positive trait, often overlooking flaws or negative behaviors. These biases profoundly impact our decision-making and judgment, influencing our interactions in ways we might not consciously be aware of. Imagine a workplace scenario where a manager consistently favors one employee, believing them to be more competent based on an initial impression. This halo effect can lead to unequal opportunities and resentment among team members, impacting morale and productivity. Addressing this bias requires conscious effort and reflection, such as implementing fair evaluation criteria and seeking input from multiple sources.

Recognizing and mitigating these biases requires intentional effort. One effective strategy is reflective questioning, which involves critically examining your assumptions. Ask yourself why you hold a particular belief and consider what evidence supports or contradicts it. This practice encourages a more balanced perspective, helping to dismantle biases before they take root.

Seeking diverse perspectives is another powerful method for countering biases. Exposing yourself to different viewpoints broadens your understanding and challenges the reinforcement circles that biases create. Engaging in discussions with people from varied backgrounds can provide fresh insights, breaking down the barriers that biases build.

In conflict resolution, awareness of biases plays a crucial role. Acknowledging biases can pave the way for more effective communication and resolution of misunderstandings. When entering mediation or negotiation, it's important to approach the situation with an open mind, recognizing your own biases and how they might color your perceptions. Techniques such as active listening and empathy can help bridge the gap between differing perspectives, fostering a more collaborative atmosphere.

Encouraging open dialogue about biases within team settings can also lead to healthier communication. Creating a safe space where biases can be discussed without judgment promotes transparency and mutual respect. This openness allows for a more honest exchange of ideas, ultimately leading to more effective and harmonious interactions.

Personal anecdotes also highlight the subtle ways biases influence our interactions. Reflect on a time when you might have misjudged someone based on first impressions or allowed confirmation bias to cloud your judgment. Recognizing these moments is the first step toward more mindful communication.

As we close this chapter, the influence of cognitive biases in communication becomes clear. We can foster more meaningful and equitable interactions by understanding, recognizing, and addressing these biases. This awareness enhances personal relationships and impacts professional environments, paving the way for a more inclusive and understanding world. As we move forward, we will explore how these insights into human behavior can be applied to strengthen your communication skills, transforming how you connect with others.

13

SUSTAINING LONG-TERM GROWTH AND CONNECTION

"If you can learn to master the art of communication, you can achieve anything you want in life." Brian Tracy

I recently overheard a group of individuals sharing their dreams and ambitions for the future. I listened to them plotting their next big move. As a coach, I know that everyone is driven by something—a dream, a purpose. These aspirations propel us forward, give us direction and motivation.

When it comes to improving your communication skills, setting clear goals can be transformative, turning vague desires into tangible milestones. Without clear goals, we risk drifting and losing sight of where we want to go. Communication goals serve as signposts, helping us confidently navigate the complexities of social and professional interactions.

I encourage you to set a short-term goal like improving your ability to engage in small talk at networking events. Defining this objective creates a specific focus, allowing for targeted practice and growth. Over time, this small goal lays the groundwork for long-term dreams, such as becoming a confident public speaker.

I've written a book about public speaking that includes many practical exercises. If you'd like to check it out scan the QR code at the back of this book.

Each short-term objective achieved, builds momentum, leading to bigger achievements. Long-term goals, like enhancing your overall communication style, provide a vision of your ultimate potential. Together, these goals form a roadmap, guiding you toward a more fulfilling and connected life.

Identifying specific, measurable goals requires thoughtful reflection. The SMART criteria offers a structured approach based on logical conscious decisions: goals should be **S**pecific, **M**easurable, **A**chievable, **R**elevant, and **T**ime-bound. For instance, instead of vaguely aiming to "improve communication skills," a SMART goal might be "to enhance listening skills by attending three workshops over the next eight weeks." This clarity makes goals more attainable and provides a clear path to follow.

However, as a coach, I know the unconscious mind can hinder SMART goals. If you don't believe the goal is achievable, you will struggle to attain it. It is important to consider the subconscious influence when setting goals. This means including emotions and internal drive when setting goals. If you read SMART backward, you will see it spells the word TRAMS. I use this acronym with clients when goal setting to go a bit deeper. TRAMS goals focus on: **T**owards, **R**elationships, **A**ttitude, **M**eaningful, **S**imple. Let me explain.

We begin by looking forward **T**owards what we want, not focusing on what we don't want, or living in the past. We rarely achieve anything on our own. Relationships are an essential ingredient in all goal-setting exercises. It is necessary to have a team of supporters and teachers to help you along the way. **A**ttitude is everything when aiming to master something new. The right attitude can help overcome any obstacle. Subconscious goals need to be **M**eaningful and **M**emorable; otherwise, we may give up too quickly or when the going gets tough. And all goals should be kept **S**imple, we tend to overcomplicate goal setting, and that can lead to overwhelm and result in a lack of goal getting.

Using the TRAMS theme, I help clients visualize their journey to achieving their goals. I ask them the following questions:

Who's driving the tram? Are you in the drivers seat taking control, or sitting up the back looking out the window?
Do you have a map of where you're going?
Do you have a schedule and are you committed to it?
Who's on the tram with you? Are they encouraging you or holding you back?
What signs will you follow along the way?
What will you do when struggling uphill?
What does your destination look like?
How will you know when you've arrived?
How will you celebrate when you get there?

When setting goals, consider different areas of your life. Professionally, you might aim to refine your presentation skills to captivate an audience. Socially, perhaps you want to expand your network by attending one event monthly. Enhancing empathy in your interactions could be a worthy pursuit. By diversifying your goals, you ensure well-rounded growth.

Track Your Progress

Tracking progress is integral to the goal-setting process. A communication journal can be invaluable, allowing you to record experiences, insights, and reflections. By documenting your journey, you gain perspective on how far you've come and what lies ahead.

Digital tools and apps can also assist in setting reminders and milestones, keeping you accountable and motivated. These tools serve as gentle nudges, ensuring you stay on track. Regularly reviewing your progress fosters a sense of accomplishment and allows you to celebrate small victories, reinforcing your commitment to growth.

Goal reflection and adjustment are crucial as you evolve. Life is dynamic, and circumstances change, requiring flexibility in your approach. By reflecting on past achievements, you gain insight into what works and needs adjustment. This process of reflection allows you to refine your goals, ensuring they remain aligned with your current needs and aspirations. Changing circumstances might prompt you to pivot or redefine your objectives. Feedback from trusted peers can also offer valuable perspectives, guiding you toward meaningful adjustments. Embracing this fluidity ensures that your goals continue to inspire and challenge you, propelling you toward a future filled with connection and growth.

Creating a Feedback Loop for Self-Improvement

A feedback loop in communication is an ongoing process of receiving, interpreting, and integrating feedback into daily interactions. Think of feedback as a diagnostic tool that highlights your strengths and identifies areas for growth. It's like a compass that helps you navigate the complex terrain of communication skills. Whether it's a nod of approval or a subtle suggestion for improvement, each piece of feedback holds potential insights. In various contexts, effective feedback methods vary. In a professional setting, structured performance reviews provide formal feedback. Yet, informal settings, like a casual chat over coffee, can offer valuable insights too, often through candid conversations with trusted colleagues or friends.

Seeking constructive feedback requires a proactive approach. It's not just about passively waiting for comments to come your way; it's about actively inviting them. Start by asking specific questions that elicit detailed responses. Instead of a broad, "How did I do?" frame your inquiry around particular aspects, like, "How can I improve my presentation skills?" This specificity encourages precise feedback, targeting areas where you seek to grow. Approach people whose opinions you respect—those who have observed your communication style. A mentor or a seasoned colleague can offer a perspective that blends experience with empathy, guiding you through constructive criticism. Their insights can illuminate blind spots and inspire new strategies for improvement.

Once you receive feedback, the challenge lies in processing and applying it constructively. It's easy to become defensive or dismissive, especially when faced with criticism. However, viewing feedback as a tool for growth can shift this perspective. Begin by analyzing the feedback for recurring themes and patterns. If multiple sources mention the same issue, it's likely an area that warrants attention. Use this analysis to create an action plan. Break down larger goals into manageable steps, focusing on one aspect at a time. For instance, if active listening is a recurring theme, you might set a goal to practice it in your next three meetings. By addressing each area incrementally, you turn feedback into a plan for refining your communication skills.

Maintaining an open mindset toward feedback is crucial. It involves letting go of ego and embracing humility. Remember, feedback is not an attack on your character but an opportunity to learn and evolve. Practicing gratitude when receiving feedback can transform the experience. Thank those who offer their insights, acknowledging the effort they put into helping you grow. This gratitude fosters a positive feedback culture, where people feel valued and are more likely to provide constructive input in the future. By cultivating this mindset, you create an environment where learning thrives, and you continuously refine your communication skills.

Fostering Long-Term Relationships with Authenticity

I mentioned the importance of authenticity in communication in chapter one and I want to talk about it again here because I believe it is the backbone of meaningful relationships, serving as the bedrock upon which trust, and connection are built. Genuine interactions are the key to creating bonds that withstand the test of time. When you approach others with sincerity, you invite them into a space where they can also be true to themselves. This mutual exchange fosters deeper connections, making both parties feel valued and understood. Authenticity lends resilience to relationships, allowing them to weather challenges and adapt to changing circumstances. Interactions become more profound without the veneer of pretense, and bonds grow deeper. Authentic behaviors, like expressing genuine concern and showing empathy, naturally strengthen these connections.

Being authentic means sharing your true self with all your strengths and vulnerabilities. This openness invites others to do the same, creating a foundation of mutual respect and understanding. Sharing personal stories and experiences builds rapport and transforms conversations from surface-level exchanges into meaningful dialogues. Practicing honesty and transparency in communication is vital. When you speak your truth, you signal trustworthiness, encouraging others to reciprocate. This transparency fosters an environment where open dialogue thrives, and differences are navigated with respect and empathy.

Despite its importance, maintaining authenticity is challenging. Social expectations and pressures often demand conformity, urging you to present a curated version of yourself. This pressure can be overwhelming, disconnecting your true self and the persona you project. To overcome this, remind yourself of the value authenticity brings. Reflect on what matters most and align your actions with those values. This alignment is a powerful antidote to external pressures. Addressing conflicts or misunderstandings with integrity is another hurdle. Authenticity in disagreements means approaching them with honesty and a willingness to listen. It involves acknowledging and learning from mistakes rather than avoiding difficult conversations. The following story of two colleagues who, despite initially clashing, forged a solid professional partnership through authenticity, is a perfect example. They learned to appreciate each other's strengths and openly discussed their differences. By embracing vulnerability and addressing conflicts head-on, they built a relationship based on mutual respect.

Story of Authenticity in Disagreements

Angela is a meticulous project manager who thrives on systems and clear deadlines. Liam is a visionary creative strategist whose ideas flow best in unstructured environments. Angela walked into her first team meeting, a notebook tucked under her arm, her list of objectives neatly outlined. The project—a high-stakes client pitch—was ambitious and under a tight deadline. As she clicked her pen and launched into an agenda, Liam leaned back in his chair, arms behind his head, a faint smirk on his face.

"Timelines are great, Angela," he interrupted, "but creativity doesn't run on a stopwatch."

Angela paused, trying to keep her voice calm. "We need structure, Liam. Without it, we'll miss the client deadline."

Liam shrugged. "I think what we need is room to think outside the box. Not box ourselves in."

The tension was palpable. Over the next few weeks, their working relationship went from strained to outright combative. Angela sent detailed follow-up emails; Liam ignored them. Liam presented incomplete ideas; Angela dismissed them. One day, after Liam turned in a half-finished concept for review, Angela lost her patience.

"This isn't acceptable, Liam!" she snapped in front of the team. "We don't have time to clean up half-baked ideas."

Liam bristled. "Maybe if you trusted me instead of treating me like an intern, I'd have the space to do my job."

The room fell silent. Both left the meeting fuming.

Later that day, their manager, Rose, pulled them into her office.

"Sit," Rose said, shutting the door. "Look, I don't expect you two to be best friends, but I need you to figure this out. Angela, Liam's ideas drive the heart of this pitch. Liam, Angela's structure makes sure we deliver it on time. If you keep working against each other, you will fail this team. So, figure it out!"

Rose's words stung—but they were true. After an awkward silence, Angela glanced at Liam. "Can we talk off the record?" Liam nodded.

"Look, I get it. I'm intense," she admitted. "I like control because, without it, I believe everything will fall apart. I've worked hard to get where I am, and I can't afford mistakes."

Liam stirred his coffee thoughtfully. "I get that. But when you micromanage, it feels like you're saying my ideas don't matter."

"That's not true," Angela said softly. "You are talented. Your concepts are brilliant—I just don't know how to fit them into a process."

Liam looked up. "And I need a process. I just don't want one that suffocates me. What if we figure out a balance?"

"What do you mean?" Angela asked.

Liam grabbed a napkin and began sketching. "You build a framework—deadlines, milestones—but leave space for me to brainstorm without hovering."

Angela nodded. "And if I need progress updates, you'll share where you're at—even if it's messy?"

"Deal."

This example illustrates how authenticity can transform potential adversaries into allies. Similarly, friendships often deepen when individuals are willing to bare their insecurities. A friend who shares their struggles invites you to do the same, forming a bond fortified by shared experiences. These relationships become sanctuaries where you can be your true self, free from judgment or pretense.

Authentic relationships thrive because they are anchored in reality. They are not built on fleeting impressions or superficial charm. Instead, they are nurtured by genuine interactions that celebrate individuality. When you embrace authenticity, you create a space where others feel seen and heard, fostering an environment of acceptance and trust. This openness encourages ongoing growth, as both parties feel safe to explore and evolve within the relationship. Authenticity is not about perfection; it's about embracing imperfections and finding beauty in them. It's about being honest, even when it's uncomfortable, and choosing connection over convenience. In a world that often prioritizes image over substance, authenticity is a refreshing reminder of what truly matters: the depth and richness of human connection.

Embracing Lifelong Learning in Communication Skills

In a rapidly changing world, the ability to adapt and grow is more important than ever. Communication, much like any other skill, requires continuous learning and evolution. It's not enough to rest on past achievements; staying open to new ideas and trends is vital for personal and professional growth. Lifelong learning keeps you adaptable and ready to meet the challenges of modern communication. It enables you to navigate diverse interactions, from virtual meetings to face-to-face conversations, with ease and confidence. By evolving your communication skills, you enrich your relationships and expand your horizons, opening doors to opportunities you might never have imagined.

People who embrace lifelong learning often actively seek knowledge, not just for its own sake but to improve how they connect with others. Think of a colleague who always brings fresh insights into team discussions or a friend who effortlessly engages people from different walks of life. These individuals exemplify the power of continuous learning. They show us that communication is not static; it's dynamic and ever-changing. By keeping their skills sharp, they inspire those around them and foster environments that thrive on collaboration and innovation. They remind us that learning doesn't stop at a certain age or stage; it's a lifelong pursuit.

Integrating learning into daily life can be a manageable task. It can be woven seamlessly into your routine, making it enjoyable and rewarding. Attending workshops or seminars is one way to gain new insights and perspectives. These events offer a platform to explore emerging trends and engage with experts in the field. But learning isn't confined to formal settings. Books, podcasts, and online courses provide a wealth of knowledge at your fingertips, allowing you to learn at your own pace. Engaging with diverse perspectives through literature or conversations broadens your understanding and enhances your communication repertoire.

Curiosity and exploration are the driving forces behind lifelong learning. They urge you to step outside your comfort zone and experiment with new communication methods and technologies. Try a new platform, like a digital collaboration tool, or converse with people from varied backgrounds. Each experience is a chance to learn, adapt, and grow. Curiosity keeps your mind agile and ready to embrace change and innovation. It challenges you to ask questions, seek answers, and explore possibilities you might not have considered before. This openness to exploration fuels your growth, propelling you toward new horizons.

To truly embrace lifelong learning, making it a core aspect of your personal and professional life is essential. Set aside regular time for skill development, treating it as a priority rather than an afterthought. Reflect on your progress, celebrate milestones, and identify areas for further growth. Setting new learning goals keeps you motivated and focused, ensuring that your communication skills continue to evolve. By committing to continuous development, you cultivate a mindset that thrives on improvement and adaptability. This commitment enhances your skills and enriches your interactions, making each conversation more meaningful and impactful.

Lifelong learning in communication is a journey without a destination. It's about the growth process, the continuous pursuit of knowledge and improvement. As you embrace this journey, you'll find that your communication skills become more refined, your connections deeper, and your understanding broader. Each step you take adds to the richness of your interactions, enhancing your personal and professional life. With each new insight and skill, you become more equipped to navigate the complexities of communication, turning challenges into opportunities for connection and growth.

14

Final Word

"Communication leads to community, understanding, intimacy and mutual valuing." Rolo May

As we reach the end of this journey together, I hope you feel a sense of empowerment in your communication abilities. The core message of this book is simple yet profound: effective communication is a skill you can learn and refine. It can transform personal and professional relationships, opening doors to deeper connections and more fulfilling interactions.

Throughout these pages, we have explored various aspects of communication, from understanding your unique style to navigating the intricacies of non-verbal cues. We've delved into the roots of social anxiety and discovered strategies to overcome it. You've learned to start conversations seamlessly and transform small talk into meaningful dialogue. We've also examined the importance of empathy, active listening, and maintaining a balance between speaking and listening.

The key takeaways from this book are designed to guide you in your everyday interactions. Remember the importance of authenticity—showing your true self builds trust and fosters genuine connections. Embrace the growth mindset; see each conversation as an opportunity to learn and improve. Apply active listening techniques and pay attention to verbal and non-verbal signals. Recognize the power of empathy in bridging gaps and creating understanding.

Now, it's time to take action. I encourage you to implement the strategies you've learned. Practice them daily, whether at work, with friends, or social gatherings. Be mindful of your communication style and strive to adapt it to different contexts. Challenge yourself to step out of your comfort zone and engage with new people. Each interaction is a chance to refine your skills and build your confidence.

Communication is a lifelong journey. It's not about reaching a destination but about continuous improvement. Embrace this journey with an open heart and a willingness to learn. The transformative impact on your life will be profound. As you grow in your communication abilities, you'll find that you can easily navigate complex social environments. You'll build strong relationships and open up new personal and professional growth opportunities.

I want to express my deepest gratitude for allowing me to guide you. Your willingness to engage with this book shows a commitment to personal development. If you're looking to take your learning further, or perhaps you're interested in personal coaching tailored to your specific needs and goals, I can help you. Scan the QR code below to get in touch.

15

MAKE A DIFFERENCE WITH YOUR REVIEW AND UNLOCK THE POWER OF CONNECTION

"Kind words don't cost much. Yet they accomplish much." Blaise Pascal

In everyday conversations, we're surrounded by moments of small talk, deep discussions, and connections that shape our lives. But there's something even more powerful that binds this world together: the joy of sharing. Just as a good story can captivate, so too can your voice leave a lasting impact.

Remember when you felt unsure about striking up a conversation or feared you wouldn't hold someone's interest? There's someone out there who feels just like that—eager to build relationships and make an impact, but unsure where to begin.

My aim with *How To Talk to Anyone: From Small Talk to Big Impact* is simple: to make the art of confident conversation accessible to all. And the only way to truly accomplish this? By reaching out to everyone.

Most people judge a book by its cover, but even more judge it by its reviews.

So, for the timid talker, the nervous networker, or the curious reader you've never met, I ask:

Could you please spare a moment to leave a review for this book?

Your review, which takes no more than a minute, could...

inspire someone to start a conversation that may change their life
provide a valuable tool for educators teaching communication skills
bring people closer together in both professional and personal spheres
empower another individual to make their own big impact with small talk.

Ready to make that difference? Just scan the appropriate QR code on the following page.

If the magic of sharing resonates with you, then you truly understand the spirit of effective communication. Welcome to the conversation. You're one of us.

With immense gratitude,

Your fellow conversationalist,

Anne McKeown

PS - There's an old saying: when you share a skill, the skill grows stronger in you. If you think this book can inspire another conversation artist, pass it along. They'll thank you, and you might just make a new friend!

USA Amazon Review Link

UK Amazon Review Link

Australia Amazon Review Link

16

REFERENCES

1. Genetic Risk Variants for Social Anxiety – PubMed
https://pmc.ncbi.nlm.nih.gov/articles/PMC5325045/

2. The Impact of Social Media on Social Anxiety
https://nationalsocialanxietycenter.com/2016/12/20/the-impact-of-social-media-on-social-anxiety/

3. Carol Dweck, Mindset. Changing the way you think to fulfil your potential
https://www.google.com.au/books/edition/Mindset_Updated

4. Mehrabian, A. (1968). Inference of attitudes from the posture, orientation, and distance of a communicator. *Journal of Consulting and Clinical Psychology, 32(3), 296–308. https://doi.org/10.1037/h0025906*

5. Jeffrey D. Karpicke and Henry L. Roediger III, titled "The Critical Importance of Retrieval for Learning," published in the journal Science in February 2008
https://www.science.org/doi/abs/10.1126/science.1152408

6. Elsa Haagensen Karlsen and Mohammed Nazar, titled "How Cultural Diversity Affects Business Communication and Collaboration" July 2024
https://www.sciencedirect.com/science/article/pii/S1877050924014406

7. Janine Willis and Alexander Todorov, titled "First impressions: making up your mind after 100 minutes exposure to a face," July 2006 *https://pubmed.ncbi.nlm.nih.gov/16866745/*

Scan for audiobook on Audible

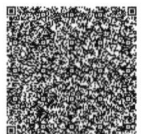

Scan for paperback on Amazon

www.ingramcontent.com/pod-product-compliance
Lightning Source LLC
Chambersburg PA
CBHW072009290426
44109CB00018B/2185